Expressing Love

Pursuing Truth

Experiencing Beauty

Three Timeless Steps
To The Ultimate Satisfaction
A Meaningful Life

Paul Hatherley

November, 2014

BALBOA
PRESS
A DIVISION OF HAY HOUSE

Balboa Press books may be ordered through booksellers or by contacting:

Balboa Press
A Division of Hay House
1663 Liberty Drive
Bloomington, IN 47403
www.balboapress.com
1-(877) 407-4847

ISBN: 978-1-4525-3584-5 (sc)
ISBN: 978-1-4525-3586-9 (hc)
ISBN: 978-1-4525-3585-2 (e)

Library of Congress Control Number: 2011910256

Printed in the United States of America

Balboa Press rev. date: 12/18/2014

Contents

Contents

FOREWORD

Have you ever observed how you respond to the simple fact of just being alive? Do you see that life offers options in how to use the short time you are alive? What options have you chosen? Most people I speak with never think about their response to being alive. Instead, they follow the patterns set by their parents, culture, and peers without consciously observing, asking questions, and discovering the options life offers.

One consequence of unconsciously adopting all the normal beliefs and purposes is at the end of our lives we often discover to our dismay that we have missed about ninety per cent of the whole show. Of course, by then it is too late to help ourselves, and also too late to help anyone else because we only have a vague feeling that we missed something important, but no clue as to precisely what it might be. As a result, each generation follows in their parent's footsteps, so as a species, we never learn how to live with *vitality, purpose, originality and meaning*.

At the heart of every vital and meaningful life is expressing love, pursuing truth, and experiencing beauty. Note, these are *activities* that require skill and awareness. This is different from the normal notion that love is a feeling, truth is acquired by osmosis, and beauty is created by nature and artistic types for our entertainment. In fact, real love, truth and beauty are accessible only by learning how to **explore and discover daily life with the purpose of understanding and nurturing**.

I

The purpose of this book is to present and contrast the two basic options life offers. First, is the *normal option* that nearly everyone chooses. In this choice people pursue security, success, approval and entertainment, while they also adopt beliefs and conclusions about politics, religion, romance, economics, and nearly every other activity in life. Second, in stark contrast, we have what I call the *conscious option.* (my personal favorite)

With the conscious option we choose to forego believing in anything, and instead learn how to observe and ask questions so we can explore life and discover what is true. Our goal is to understand the complexity of ordinary experience so we can nurture ourselves, other people, and nature. A lifetime of vitality is found in this process. Now, we spend our lives engaged in the risky internal adventure of exploring both the ordinary and the extraordinary for the *purpose of discovering* what is true.

Contrast this *conscious option* with the *normal choice* of creating a secure internal life by adopting ideas and beliefs to cover every aspect of life, so rather than exploring and discovering, we spend our lives defending and explaining, or lapsing into oblivion and complacency, while never learning anything new. Just by the sound of it, what seems more vital, original and meaningful to you — observing and asking questions so you can *explore* life and *discover* what is true — or defending, explaining and justifying your ideas, beliefs and conclusions?

Right now I am speaking intellectually, but as we go thru the process of exploring these two responses to life, it may become obvious that the conscious option is a truly big deal, not just for each individual, but literally, the whole human species.

II

About now you may be thinking that in offering just two options, *conscious vs. normal,* I am being more than a little black and white about this issue. The truth is that within each option there is nearly an infinite number of variations in how we can apply them. Not only that, but we often blend the two options, so we may have a *scientific side* that we apply when studying nature and the physical world, but then rely on *beliefs and feelings* when dealing with everything else: like romance, politics, religion, economics, parenting, personal fulfillment, etc.

The scientific method, where we observe facts, ask questions, and then apply reason and experiments rather than rely on beliefs or feelings to *understand reality* is relatively new. In the few hundred years we have utilized the scientific method to understand nature it has been breathtaking in its consequences in terms of our technological advancements. One tiny problem is that *internally,* in terms of our collective mental and emotional development, we still live in caves, paint graffiti on the walls, and scratch our armpits as we swing thru the trees.

A second problem is we do not acknowledge this internal backwardness, but imagine, or feel that *external* technological advances mean that we are also *internally* sophisticated. When we believe that a superior internal development is a logical and inevitable consequence of external advancement, we instantly create a glaring *contradiction* between the *image* of ourselves, and the observable *facts of reality.*

A second purpose of this book is to heal the contradiction between our image and the facts by providing information that will illuminate the real degree of internal human development.

III

What I do differently in this book from what has been done before is I apply the scientific method — observing facts, asking questions, applying reason and experimenting — to the task of understanding and mastering internal needs and potentials. The difference between my work and strict science is I do not rely on mathematics or do blind studies. What I do is apply a *scientific attitude* to the problem of defining mental and emotional development, internal fulfillment, and lasting happiness.

The process begins with defining in *experiential* terms, **not** vague ideas or silly sentiments, precisely what my words mean, so anyone who wants to learn the definitions can test their validity by observing his own experience over time. This is not strictly *scientific* in terms of being mathematically proven, but it does offer a new approach where we shift from *arguing* what we *feel or believe* to comparing, contrasting and *discussing* what we *observe and experience*.

If we bring an innocent honesty and integrity to the task, then we will learn about ourselves, life and other people. If we do not, then nothing will touch or teach us anyway, mathematically proven or not. After all, there are still people in these United States who fervently believe the Earth is flat and cite the Holy Bible as offering *proof,* and I would never want to intrude on anyone's beliefs trying to convince them otherwise.

Instead, I offer a process for *expressing love, pursuing truth and experiencing beauty* that over time leads to *developing wisdom.* The process necessary to master *love, truth, beauty and wisdom* feeds our deepest *internal needs,* and also fulfills those uniquely *human potentials* necessary to create lasting happiness.

In my experience as a teacher of internal development, I have seen that most people are not trained to observe, think about, and understand their *internal* needs and potentials. Instead, they choose to blindly follow impulses and desires. This means few people differentiate the *lasting satisfaction* of feeding real needs, from the *temporary pleasure* of gratifying desires.

It is important to note that if we fail to distinguish between *lasting satisfaction* and *temporary pleasure*, then *meaning* is not an issue we can even think about. If we do discern the differences between pleasure and satisfaction, we can create a *working definition* that says **meaning** *is a natural consequence of any life-affirming experience that provides* **enduring value.**

Now you might ask, "If I learn to master internal needs and potentials, will this create lasting satisfaction that has enduring value? To answer this question, we first need to master the three activities of expressing love, pursuing truth and experiencing beauty, and then note whether or not we create lasting satisfaction and enduring value, i.e. *a meaningful life.*

My hypothesis states that to create the enduring value necessary for a meaningful life requires that we **fulfill our internal potential to express love, pursue truth, and experience beauty until we integrate all three into our consciousness and behavior and develop wisdom.**

To accomplish this task requires that we first define love, truth, and beauty in enough detail to create a clear mental picture of each activity. The following working definitions are designed to create a first sketch, or *working definition* by clarifying specific characteristics natural to each one.

V

<u>Working Definitions for Love, Truth & Beauty</u>

<u>**Love**</u>—is a caring *response* to being alive—not a *reaction* to the excitement stimulated by gratifying lust, greed, or desire. Love requires commitment and surrender—it is never half-hearted or divided. *Love requires giving our whole-hearted energy and attention with a willingness to learn, change, and even suffer for the innocent purpose of becoming competent to understand and nurture everything we love.*

<u>**Truth**</u>—requires we *observe* facts, and then use *reason* and *caring* to discover what they *mean*, which we test over time until we accumulate insight and create *understanding.* Truth is **not** a sentimental feeling, intellectual theory, or spiritual intuition.

<u>**Beauty**</u>—is experienced through the innocent expression of truth and love, and the varied creations found in nature, books, movies, art and music. Beauty is a fulfillment of our senses, *never* an assault; and beauty is always in harmony with truth and love, *never* in conflict.

Does it seem that as defined here love, truth, and beauty are *timeless*, and if integrated into daily life would build lasting value and permanent meaning in anyone's life? If you honestly see that love, truth, and beauty are essential, do you *want* your experience of everyday life to contain the *enduring value* necessary for a meaningful life badly enough to work for it?

Clearly answering these questions will help identify where you stand on two critical issues necessary to create internal fulfillment. That is, you must first observe the *need* for love, truth, and beauty; and then you must *want* the work, risk, and change necessary to master all three.

Many people think they want to grow, but find that when offered a clearly defined avenue for growth, they do **not** *want* the work and real change that are pre-requisites for all internal development. In normal life, the lack of an experiential definition for even one internal need or potential makes it possible to hide behind a *belief* we want to grow, when in *fact* we are too entrenched in our internal habits and patterns to move an inch.

If you really want to grow, and your common sense says that mastering love, truth, and beauty is a good place to begin, then you will love the clarity created by an observation based, reason enhanced, precisely defined, and truly caring picture of internal development. If you do **not** want to grow, then no degree of clarity will be powerful enough to disturb the inertia of a normal belief-based status quo.

In fact, it is not the purpose of this book to disturb anyone's status quo. Instead, it is the purpose of this book to answer several critical questions. We have already asked two essential questions. The first, "Can I see that I *need* to master love, truth, and beauty?" The second, "Do I *want* the work, risk, and internal change required to master love, truth, and beauty?"

The third question, "*How* do I integrate the timeless activities of love, truth, and beauty into daily life?" All three questions are addressed throughout this book, sometimes directly, and sometimes indirectly. In answering these questions our understanding of life, ourselves, and other people is expanded in ways we could not anticipate, but may discover creates an internal journey thru life with enough risk, change and genuine adventure to make the experience truly vital and meaningful!

It is a fact that human beings have complex brains and emotions that create a potential for developing understanding and caring that is greater than any other animal. We also have a longer life span than most animals. Together, our brains, emotions, and life spans provide an opportunity for internal development that other animals do not possess.

Mastering the experience of *love, truth, beauty and wisdom* is necessary to fulfill our human potentials. As a species, we have failed to consciously pursue and master these four activities well-enough to master internal development. Perhaps, we have been too absorbed by survival needs to truly care about our potentials, which helps explain why we often view internal development as a luxury we may get around to one day when we have enough surplus time and money, and feel secure.

The problem is that technology has given us the power to exploit the earth and each other so totally that if love, truth, and beauty are **not** soon seen as necessities, we could make survival impossible. Even if we survive, we are now immersed in the process of making the quality of life so *internally* impoverished and empty of meaning that survival may not matter.

What does matter is that we learn how to build the skill, awareness, and caring necessary to make our individual lives internally satisfying, and then use our understanding to build institutions—political, economic, environmental, social and educational—that are *consciously designed* to enhance and fulfill everyone's life experience, rather than operate as mechanisms to protect an entrenched status quo that is too often exploitive, impersonal and self-destructive, rather than life-affirming.

Up to now, love, truth, and beauty have been *self-guiding principles of life* to a few people, and *sentimental ideals* to most. What we need is to clearly define the *internal processes* required to make love, truth, and beauty *experiential activities* that can be learned by anyone who sees the benefit and wants the work of mastering these timeless steps to internal fulfillment.

My interest in fulfilling my internal potentials began at the age of 5, when my grandmother died. She was the only person who cared about me, and her death sent me on a lifelong mission to learn what would make life meaningful.

When I was 5 it was 1950, and the United States had a population one-third the size it is now. Also, in elementary school my history books described the United States as having "limitless" resources. My world felt *externally* safe, but when my grandmother died it became *internally* empty. So my quest for meaning was a response to my circumstances and preferences.

In the ensuing sixty-five plus years since I was 5, the world has changed dramatically. Now, instead of a little over 2 billion human beings on the planet, there are over seven billion! Instead of resources being *unlimited*, we are frantically scrambling to exploit what remains of Earth's resources, hoping to make it through our lifetimes before we in the United States suffer like much of the rest of the world has always suffered.

What these changes mean is that we need to develop our minds and emotions, master love, truth, beauty and wisdom, and create individual lives that are satisfying and meaningful. Then, we can *think* about our own and the world's problems competent to *see reality accurately* and define every real *need and potential* without the distortions created by judgments, beliefs, opinions, egos, or superficial sentiments.

Right now all we need to do is watch the nightly news, any channel, for even a few days to see that human interactions are characterized by a cacophony of competing egos, advantages, belief systems, philosophies, theories, and manipulative tactics. Neither understanding nor mastery of love, truth, beauty and wisdom are what we see on the news, or in the attitudes and actions of our political, economic, and educational institutions. Instead, what we see is a desperate need for internal development on every level of human life — from our individual lives to cultural institutions, to global purposes and behaviors.

Whether we are motivated to grow to benefit ourselves alone, for our families, or for ourselves, families, and the benefit of all human beings, it is important that we recognize the need for internal development. Acknowledging and feeding this need will provide a degree of internal fulfillment and permanent meaning that nothing else in human life can offer.

Of course, my saying this does not make it true. So if you read this book and master the definitions, insights and skills, and then apply them in your daily life, you will see for yourself what is true, as well as satisfying and meaningful.

My purpose is to present all the information necessary to create a daily *experience* of *expressing love, pursuing truth, experiencing beauty and developing wisdom.* These activities define a precise path to the internal satisfaction, permanent meaning, and lasting happiness that human beings have always longed for, but have rarely had the opportunity to create or experience.

Part One

Introduction To

Love, Truth & Beauty

Paul Hatherley

Love is the Source of Vitality & Meaning

Love is a complicated human need and experience. There are few needs in everyday life that cause more intense feelings of longing, insecurity, and desire than our hunger to be loved. At the same time, there are also few experiences that cause more confusion, disillusion, or even bitterness. Ask anyone about her experience with love and you will hear a story of excitement, hope, pain, longing, fear, fulfillment, and sometimes, deep disappointment.

Normally, people assume that love is something they are supposed to *feel,* or *receive* from another person. Rarely is anyone aware that love requires mastering specific skills and awareness before it can be experienced or expressed. If we ever do think about expressing love, it is usually in terms of what we can offer *externally* (money, food or services), rather than as something we need to give *internally* (energy, innocent interest, and genuine understanding).

The first step toward becoming competent to *express* love is to consciously explore ordinary events from past and present until we can define the *experience* of love. With normal training, love is often seen as a mysterious reaction. For instance, when we react to someone by feeling a mysterious chemistry, desire, lust, etc., we sometimes characterize this reaction by saying, "I have fallen *in love!*"

On the other hand, less mysterious is when we react to a gratifying object or experience and describe our reaction by saying, "I just *love* my car, house, steak, movie, etc." Often, we define love as the feeling of attachment we experience toward a person or object that has pleased us, or we anticipate might please or fulfill us.

Love at first sight is an experience that happens when *at a glance* we anticipate an object or person will be especially gratifying. So when a person is really hot looking, or appears to be introspective, kindly, or even dangerous (depending on our preferences), we can react instantly and mysteriously by *falling in love.*

Love as a Response to Being Alive

Has there ever been a time when for one unguarded and startlingly clear moment you stood outside yourself and observed you really are alive, and terrifyingly enough, really are going to die? I have had these moments. The first was on the shores of Lake Michigan at a family picnic with grandparents, cousins, aunts, uncles, etc. I was about seven, and was sitting on the shore as the sun went down.

I was mesmerized by the gentle lapping of the small waves, and by the fading light reflecting off the sand making it appear flecked with thousands of tiny grains of glittering gold. In that moment, I was acutely aware of being alive and alone, and it became terrifyingly clear that I too would go through a lifespan and die.

This experience was the first of many where my awareness of being alive was so palpable that it frightened me. At times, I have tried to cling to this awareness, but sadly discovered that like all life's experiences, it too fades. The lesson is that life is in constant motion and we can cling to nothing, and if we try to stop the flow with our judgments, opinions or beliefs, we make it impossible to experience the mystery and wonder of just being alive.

We can easily miss life by never allowing ourselves to engage the mystery and feel the fear an acute awareness of being alive has the power to create. Protecting ourselves from reality only leads to dulling our senses and diminishing our vitality. Another consequence of avoiding reality is that we act *as if* we have an infinite amount of time, so we never feel a *sense of urgency*, and nothing really matters. While we all intellectually know we are mortal, we often form daily priorities as if we are never going to die.

Acting as if our time is unlimited is just one of countless ways we routinely avoid reality and choose fantasy. This choice is so common that it is a *normal* response to being alive. One problem with choosing fantasy over reality is that we kill curiosity, and make love impossible. On the other hand, if we choose to acknowledge that we are alive, and also the proud possessors of a lifespan that is never guaranteed beyond the current breath, we have sound reasons to respond to life determined to *love* every moment.

To make love our primary response to everyday life, we must first define the *experience*, and then identify the precise purposes and actions necessary to *express* love. If you remember, we first defined love in the **Foreword**:

Love — is a caring *response* to being alive — not a *reaction* to the excitement stimulated by lust, greed, or desire. Love requires a whole-hearted commitment and a willingness to suffer. *This means that real love requires we give our whole-hearted energy and attention with a desire to learn, change and even suffer for the purpose of becoming competent to understand and nurture.*

How to put this definition into practice in ordinary life? A good place to start is by identifying priorities. In normal life it is common for security, success, entertainment and approval to be our primary priorities. The energy for these priorities is created and maintained by *believing* they will make us happy. However, if we observe everyday life, we quickly see that security is not possible for a mortal being, success does not feed internal needs, approval can never build self-worth, and entertainment may work fine as a way to pass time, but it does not provide satisfaction or meaning.

On the other hand, if we become whole-hearted about mastering *self-awareness, life-awareness and other-awareness,* we build bridges of understanding that connect us to life and other people. At the same time that we develop understanding, we also master the skill to feed and fulfill internal needs and potentials. *A loving response to life can be defined in part as a whole-hearted commitment to develop self-life & other-awareness, and to master nurturing.*

Self-Awareness vs. Self-Absorption

In normal life almost everyone is *self-absorbed*, while very few people develop *self-awareness*. How can we tell the difference? Actually, it is quite easy. Self-awareness leads to developing the awareness and skills necessary to feed and fulfill internal **and** external needs and potentials. By contrast, self-absorption is a natural consequence of *obsessing* about our image, advantage, or security with an attitude that is not interested in understanding reality, internal needs and potentials, ordinary life, or other people.

One reason that spiritual concepts and new-age fantasies are so popular is they encourage us to *feel*, or *believe* we are on the cutting edge of consciousness, when in fact, we are self-absorbed and disconnected from our experience of everyday life. By contrast, if we want to measure our level of self-awareness we can observe to what degree we have, or have not mastered our internal needs and potentials.

This insight reveals that a high degree of *self-awareness* will create a high degree of competence to feed needs and fulfill potentials. We can also measure our self-awareness by other consequences — the degree of lasting satisfaction and genuine meaning we routinely create in everyday life.

How does someone build self-awareness? Very easy, every day we *observe* ordinary experiences, record our *responses*, and acknowledge the *consequences*. Please note this process requires we *observe facts*, rather than rely on beliefs and feelings. Perhaps, not quite as easy as it sounds!

Developing Self-Awareness

It is impossible to love ourselves or life when we understand little or nothing about either one! This is a critical insight because most people believe they can love themselves, life, children, mates and friends, even though they rarely, or never pay attention to internal experiences, and as a result, understand little or nothing about their own or anyone else's *motivations, purposes, needs, wants, attitudes, choices and behaviors.*

Without self-awareness, we spend our lives reacting to survival needs, procreating, and entertaining ourselves until one day we just fall off a cliff into an eternal black abyss. We call this sad process, *a normal life.* Essentially, except for the entertainment, any discerning person would find it difficult to distinguish between a normal human life and the life of any other species of mammal on the planet.

What then is the first step for anyone who wants to develop self-awareness? Step one is to *observe, think about, and explore* daily experiences, thoughts, and conversations. To begin, all we have to do is just listen—to ourselves! Surprisingly, most people do not pay attention and listen to either what they think, or say, and consequently fail to notice when they have a significant topic to explore versus babbling along, until somehow, they hope a significant point or conversation will just magically appear.

In addition to listening to what we say, we also need to observe our thoughts. Together, what we think about and verbalize reveals our purposes, what we care about, and the degree we understand ourselves versus being clueless.

What do you see is true in your thoughts and conversations? Do you think and talk about love, truth, and beauty, as well as internal needs, purposes, potentials, and motivations so you become not only self-aware, but also life-aware? In observing your thoughts and conversation, do you see where you are contradictory versus congruent? Have you learned how to make a conversation satisfying and meaningful for both yourself and another person?

As you ask and answer these questions, your awareness of internal life will increase. In identifying purposes, for instance, you observe priorities and learn what you care about. This establishes a base line you can grow from. Also, after identifying your purposes and what you care about you can see whether your current priorities create satisfaction and meaning, or if they lead to internal emptiness devoid of any real fulfillment. With this knowledge, you have the power to make real changes or *stay the course.* Either way, you are more self-aware.

Another important increase in self-awareness happens when we observe areas of contradiction. ***Contradictions are created when behaviors conflict with intentions, desires contradict needs, beliefs contradict facts, and those times when we are especially neurotic and our beliefs and feelings contradict each other, and reality!***

Seeing our contradictions adds an important piece to the puzzle of self-awareness. Normally, we can see internal conflict and hypocrisy in other people with laser like 20/20 vision, but are totally myopic in seeing ourselves. Healing this discrepancy by observing ourselves accurately makes real internal growth both appealing and possible.

Another insight critical to self-awareness is to see the difference between *thinking* about an issue until we create understanding, and *obsessing* in mental circles. In normal life, we assume that obsessing in circles counts as thinking. People often say, "I have been thinking about x for days, but I just don't know what to do...feel, choose, etc.

The point is that if our thinking is based on exploring a topic using observation and reason, then our understanding will increase. On the other hand, if what we call *thinking* relies on ideas, feelings or beliefs that circle our brains but forever fail to identify the critical facts, or discover precisely what we need, then this qualifies as *obsessing*. The normal concept of thinking is a frustrating process where we obsess in circles over conflicting feelings and beliefs, argue needs against wants, or pit one desire against another and never understand a single thing.

What is your process? Do you pay attention to your thoughts and conversation and *think about* and explore the significant issues until you understand — in detail — your own or someone else's motivations, purposes, and needs? Or do you *obsess* about events or feelings and fail to make progress in your understanding and internal competence?

It matters less how you respond to these two questions than that you answer them innocently and honestly. It will take effort and integrity to answer each question, not just once, but over time, so you gather layer upon layer of insight and gradually increase your self-awareness. *A loving response to being alive requires accurate observations and intelligent questions that lead to real understanding.*

Reacting vs. Responding

There are many avenues to developing self-awareness, and observing our thoughts and conversations is a good place to begin. Continuing on this path, we can observe that every event in daily life elicits either a *reaction* or a *response*, and there are always *consequences*. I define *reactions* as being *unconscious* choices. By contrast, I characterize *responses* as *conscious* choices made with self-awareness, and a genuine desire to understand what is needed.

Both processes are easy to observe. For instance, if in fact you fail to eat all day it is likely that by dinner you will be famished, and may *react* by overeating (assuming you do not suffer from anorexia, etc.). If you do this day after day, the consequence may well be that your health is diminished, your energy becomes unstable, and you may gain a lot of weight. On the other hand, if you observe the critical facts, understand the issues, and care about the consequences, then you can *respond* by *consciously choosing* to eat at regular intervals throughout the day.

This example is simple, but the process of thinking is the same for every event of daily life, simple or complex, minor or major. For instance, if you are criticized or rejected by someone you love, what do you do? Most people *unconsciously react* and never learn how to *consciously respond* with a desire to explore and understand. This is one way we create neurotic patterns that never change.

The major difference between reacting and responding is that when we react to events our purpose is to control, which means we want to protect against feeling pain and maximize pleasant feelings. When reacting, it is not our *purpose* to learn from positive and negative experiences so we expand our understanding. In stark contrast, when we *respond* to life, our *purpose changes from wanting control to wanting to understand*, which means we consciously work to learn from every event, painful or not.

Shifting away from wanting control and toward a desire to understand is the single most significant step in developing self-awareness. Without this shift we may *try to grow,* but will always be handicapped—because we do not *want* to understand. So how does this work in daily life?

Imagine a time when you felt unfairly criticized, or were rejected by someone you loved, did you *unconsciously react,* or *respond* with a *conscious purpose*? If you reacted, then it is likely you were hurt and angry, and then justified yourself while blaming the other person. If you responded, then it is likely you tried to understand the *grain of truth* in the criticism or rejection. As a result, you would also try to define your role in creating the painful circumstances.

When we respond rather than react to painful events, our *purpose* is to *learn about ourselves, life, and other people;*

and in the process expand our understanding of precisely what is needed to make all our interactions both satisfying and meaningful. Does this mean we don't grieve when we lose someone we love? Absolutely not, because real loving requires caring without defending ourselves, so when someone we love rejects us, we inevitably experience pain.

The point is that self-awareness is not intended to make us invincible, rather it is intended to help us become internally fulfilled by acquiring the mental and emotional development necessary to become *loving and wise*. This is the exact opposite of what people normally want. Normally, we want to *control* every pain, and as a result, become manipulative and protective. In stark contrast, in pursuing love and wisdom we become innocent and vulnerable.

Just what reactions and responses must you observe to become more self-aware? All of them, but here are a few specifics. For one, you need to notice how you spend discretionary time. Do you choose activities based solely on having fun, or do you choose activities you can learn from and will be meaningful? Even when choosing activities strictly to pass time, do you pay attention to each activity with a *conscious purpose* of wanting to learn about yourself and other people, or do you focus primarily on pleasure?

What do you suppose is the likely consequence if you concentrate on daily life wanting to learn rather than control or entertain? One consequence may be that you discover your normal training is inadequate in almost every area of *meaningful* activity — such as feeding internal needs, exploring significant issues to the point of understanding, structuring a conversation so it is satisfying for both yourself and another person, becoming competent to build self-worth in yourself or a child, or being able to build genuine emotional bonds with a mate, child, or friend.

This brings us to the biggest obstacle to self-awareness. That is, most people will not tolerate acknowledging and exploring their personal inadequacies, and then *respond* by wanting to *grow, change,* and become *internally competent.* Instead, most people deny or explain away inadequacies, and at the same time, find ways to blame someone else.

Acknowledging our inadequacies is painful, but if we want to grow it is something we must get over. Being able to observe precisely where we are ignorant and inadequate is simply part of becoming a real adult. However, we are so often insecure in our value that we rarely admit a single specific inadequacy, which is one reason few people become internal adults developmentally competent to take responsibility for their ignorance and mistakes.

The good news is that if we replace our fear of being inadequate with *consciously working* to become self-aware, then we will develop our minds and emotions and become internally competent—and over time—loving and wise. Mental and emotional development creates the self-worth and internal fulfillment all of us crave, but in normal life we simply do not have the training to create.

Becoming loving, wise, and internally fulfilled is the most meaningful reward life offers, and one obstacle we need to overcome is to accept that our egos are going to suffer criticisms and changes. One inevitable criticism we can look forward to discovering is that we are far less internally developed than we had hoped, or imagined, and certainly less than we would like anyone else to observe.

Perhaps you can see that self-awareness is not something you can acquire in a day. On the other hand, you can start the process right now by answering the questions we have posed, and then begin to *observe, think about, and learn from everyday life.*

Life-Awareness

It can be startling to see how people can live a long time but learn little or nothing about life. The problem is that most people believe they can learn about life just by living for a long time. This creates the idea that if we live to be old, then we will also become wise. The ever popular theory of *learning by osmosis* often handicaps and retards our developmental progress. The sad truth is that without training, we spend our life's time unconsciously reacting to events, and it is not our intention to give energy and interest to understanding life in all its joy and pain, fulfillment and frustration, happiness and tragedy.

Similar to self-awareness, life-awareness requires becoming whole-hearted, totally committed, and eager to experience the heights of joy and depths of despair with a burning desire to learn from both. While developing self-awareness focuses on *internal* reality — life-awareness focuses on the *external*. Both areas of awareness are needed if we want to master *loving* every moment of being alive.

Focusing on life begins with *observing* that life is bigger than we are, and more important. One of the first things we see is the universe is divided into two entities, our little selves and a whole world of options and objects called life. If we remain self-absorbed, we never accept even this fact. Instead, we go through life acting as if we are the center of the universe, so our own desires, fears, beliefs, ideas and judgments are all we ever really think or care about.

On the other hand, when we accept that the universe has a separate existence, then a loving response is to pay attention and learn what life offers, and requires. With this information, we develop the awareness to make choices in harmony with our needs and potentials, and we provide the focused attention necessary to understand ourselves, other people, and some of life's options and mysteries.

What does life offer? This is a question I have been asking and answering all my life. For instance, in my early twenties, I met a man who was a concert pianist and liked to talk. His two favorite subjects were himself and music. I knew nothing about classical music, but knew enough to see that it had been around for a long time, it was a sensual art that contained both intellectual meaning and emotional impact, and it seemed to contain a mysterious *intrinsic and enduring value* that I wanted to experience and understand.

So I hung around this guy for months listening to him. He was a narcissistic person (aren't we all?) and loved to talk about himself, but he also loved classical music and liked to talk about that too. For the price of listening but rarely speaking, I learned about classical music — the composers and instruments, as well as the forms — symphonies, concertos, sonatas, etc. He also introduced me to the most beautiful works and best conductors and soloists.

One consequence of this education is that I learned to love classical music, and I have listened to it daily ever since. This daily experience has provided comfort, insight, inspiration, and a conscious bridge to both life and beauty.

Also, during this time when I was new to the adult world and looking to see what life offered, I observed that I needed to explore nature because she is the source of our existence, real, and free of the artificial protections offered in the city. It seemed essential to master being in nature if I wanted to *experience* and *love* life.

Like with music, I began by gathering information, so I got books on trees, flowers, birds, animals, geography, etc. I also needed to become competent to take care of myself in nature, so I learned how to use a compass and read topographical maps, backpack for weeks at a time, etc. Then, I set out to practice being in nature by myself.

One thing I quickly discovered is that when backpacking alone, especially when being three days in and not able to pack out in a day, the feeling of aloneness can be excruciating, especially at night. A *palpable* feeling of being alive, alone, and terrifyingly fragile would lie across my mind like an oppressive blanket that was hard to shake off.

At the same time I felt terrified, I learned that in fact there is no real danger, only an intense awareness of being alive and alone. Another awareness was seeing how empty I felt, how little I understood, and how very large and mysterious life really is. When distracted by the city this awareness was largely unavailable, but when alone in the mountains it hit my consciousness like a brick wall.

Being in nature and experiencing the solitude, beauty, and daily risk and adventure provides a satisfying contrast to the safe predictability of city life where every conceivable service is always at our fingertips. Over time, becoming competent to be alone in nature can create a degree of both *self-awareness* and *self-reliance* that may be difficult or even impossible to obtain any other way.

What you can see is that I sought life with the *conscious purpose* of wanting to discover concrete ways to observe, learn about, experience, and love her. Music and nature were two avenues I chose to enhance my life-awareness. It does not matter what avenues you choose, the point is that you need to *consciously pursue life*, rather than *passively* wait for life to somehow find and fulfill you.

Life is shy, and wants to be pursued and loved, she is never the aggressor. So if we expect life to find us, it is important to see this is **not** going to happen. Of all that life offers, the two most significant options are that we can be *passively normal* and pursue security, success, approval, and entertainment, or we can *consciously choose* to explore life's options and master every internal need and potential.

These are two options that life has always offered, but people have rarely identified, and to my knowledge, before now have never even tried to defined in precise detail. Once we are aware of our choices, then a loving response requires that we master love, truth, beauty and wisdom. As a choice, it's really a no-brainer! *The reason is that all internal fulfillment and enduring happiness is a natural consequence of mastering these four internal activities.*

It is important to notice that the internal development necessary to *express love, pursue truth, experience beauty and develop wisdom*, represents an evolution in awareness and skill that is complicated and requires information, study, and time. My books provide the necessary information, while every reader must contribute the time and effort to observe, study, apply reason and experiment until he/she understands the material in terms of actual life experience.

Other-Awareness

It can be a shock to discover that you and the universe are two – not one! In spite of what all the new-age and spiritual gurus promise, you are **not** going to return to the womb, which was the first and last time you will ever be *one with the universe*. So your sole opportunity to be one with the universe has already happened, you mostly slept through it and missed it, and it will never happen again. Oh well, too bad so sad.

I can afford to be flippant about this loss because I

never had the normal *one with the universe* experience. Instead, my mother was a self-absorbed and truly inadequate person who supported me *externally* while I was in the womb (because nature did not give her a choice), but early on through some form of placental communication let me know I was on my own *internally*. This meant that if I wanted love, then I would have to provide it for myself.

It was a long time ago and I cannot recall my exact response, but I vaguely remember processing the information, shedding a tear or two, and then accepting the facts. When it was finally time to go, I came down the chute with my fists clenched, my eye on the door, and ready to fend for myself.

Good thing too, because for the first ten days my mother had pneumonia, so I was left alone in the baby lounge. I still had a good time flirting with the nurses, but my fetal and neo-natal experience made it clear that I was all alone in this new world. The only up-side of being alone and responsible is that you are also, *in charge!*

All in all, I had a very productive fetal and neo-natal career. While all the other kids were having a good time in their mother's bellies and came out passive, I had real-life experience and came out determined to be independent. This early training left several career opportunities open to me. I could have used these early experiences as training to become a serial killer, or instead, be inspired to love life while also nurturing myself and other people. Fortunately for me, and maybe the world, I chose the latter.

As you can see in the previous story, I tried to use a little humor to play with and lighten the serious facts. The point of the story is that my parents were unavailable internally, and I grew up hungry for conscious connections. I *responded* to my hunger by *giving* other people the energy, interest and understanding that I longed to receive. One motivation for developing other-awareness can be created primarily from just feeling intensely alive and alone, and then *giving* the energy and interest we want to receive.

With normal priorities, most people repress their longings hoping they can avoid the pain that comes from being hungry for the *internal satisfaction* their intimate relationships fail to offer. The problem is that when we avoid the pain caused by our internal hungers, we can never acquire the information necessary to learn what other people need, or even what we need, and as a result, we are forever unable to master loving life, ourselves, or other people.

Other-awareness requires we consciously observe that we and the universe are not one, but two. Then, we must use the pain of loneliness to create a burning desire to see, understand, and nurture all life. *The combination of learning, understanding, and nurturing is a loving response: whether in our own lives, or for other people and nature.*

When a loving response to being alive becomes integrated into daily life, then developing a burning desire for *self-life and other-awareness* is a natural consequence that prepares us to move forward in our internal development and learn the gentle art of *pursuing truth*.

Paul Hatherley

Pursuing Truth

Like life and love, truth too is elusive and will not reveal herself unless we actively pursue her over time. Pursuing truth is like pursuing the Holy Grail in the Camelot stories. The Knights of the Round Table would go on a mission to find the Grail, but only a knight *pure-in-heart* could both find and touch it without being killed. I first read these stories as a teenager and immediately felt guilty and ashamed because already, I did not feel qualified to both find and touch the Grail.

The reason, as I considered it, was that I was way too lustful to qualify as pure-in-heart. Not only was I lustful, but as a child, I once got caught stealing some candy, and there were a few other times when I did not get caught, so in my mind I was clearly not qualified to pursue the Grail. Still, over the years I kept thinking about what pure-in-heart might really mean.

Eventually, it came to me that my idea of pure-in-heart was based on a Christian ideal that required perfect adherence to the prevailing rules. With a little observation, I saw that some people seemed to follow the rules but were mean-spirited, and in my estimation not the least bit loving or wise. So, on rethinking the whole issue it seemed that pure-in-heart really required being *innocently honest* about every strength and weakness, *vulnerable* to love, loss, and pain, and *whole-hearted* and *responsible* in pursuing truth—in good times and bad.

While I may have been self-serving in that I re-defined pure-in-heart so I could qualify (you be the judge here), I did eventually create a definition that offered a more human, attainable, and compassionate view of the internal qualities necessary to be pure-in-heart. The point is that if we want to pursue truth and get to know her personally and intimately, we must become whole-hearted in our desire to see ourselves, life, and other people accurately and as is, without the usual distortions provided by normal beliefs, feelings, judgments, fears or desires. Very simple.

Well, maybe not so simple. My first real experience with the price of pursuing truth came at the ripe old age of 8. For some time, I had noticed that my parents did not treat me as if they cared about me. For instance, they would say "no" to innocent activities when there was clearly no reason for it. They would also give birthday or Christmas presents they obviously put no thought or effort into, and sometimes gave me things that were broken, old, or simply unusable.

So I thought about the issue, and when I had a number of what I thought were irrefutable examples, confronted my parents with the statement, "I don't think you love me." What I expected was they would be concerned that I felt unloved, and would ask about the source of my sad conclusion, so I would then have the opportunity to present my case.

Instead, they reacted as if I were criticizing them, and retaliated by saying I was being "disrespectful", and then demanded I retract my statement. I refused, and was hit with the belt and sent to my room to spend the night without dinner. The next day everything external returned to normal, and the subject was never brought up again.

Internally, however, I was never the same. My parents confirmed my worst suspicions and more. What I could see was that at age 8, and even in my mind *only a little boy*, I wanted to see and understand what was true between my parents and me, but they did not want to understand anything. Instead, they were not curious about either the truth or my perspective, they only wanted to pretend everything was ok, and they wanted me to make them feel good as parents. It was clear that the punishment for not making them feel good was disapproval and pain.

Bottom line, not only was I not loved, I was alone in wanting to understand the truth about myself, parents, life, death, love, and meaning. The next day, my collie dog and I walked into the woods near my house. Once alone, I put my arms around his furry neck and sobbed out my feelings of being alive and alone without a friend. *Life was teaching me about the price of pursuing truth.*

I was also learning that pursuing truth is not some mystical, magical, philosophical, religious, or intellectual fantasy. Instead, pursuing truth is an intensely personal, painfully real, and truly passionate experience where joy is always accompanied by sadness, and vice-versa.

There was a ray of joy in the experience with my parents because I learned that even at 8, I had the internal power to stand alone, pay the price, and pursue the truth.

The significance of this story is that people have taught me over the years that everyone's experience is similar to mine in that we all experience a price for pursuing truth. One part of the price is opting out of pretending, and instead, choosing to see ourselves, life, and other people *as is*, positive and negative. This is akin to being the only sober person at a drunken party! Sometimes we experience a strong temptation to get as toasted as everyone else—just so we can feel that we fit in and belong.

I have given myself the option to get drunk and join the normal party of life on more than one occasion. What life has taught me, however, is that pretense always comes up being *internally* empty and devoid of meaning, no matter how *externally* pleasant it may feel in the moment. Since life ends in death, and pleasantness without truth ultimately becomes excruciatingly painful, my choice has been to pursue truth and go toward internal meaning. Which choice appeals to you?

Facts + Meaning=Truth

If you are still reading, does this mean that pursuing truth has some appeal? Well, don't be frightened, you can learn *about* the truth and still never pursue or experience it! Once you want the truth, however, the next step is to define what you are looking for, so you have a chance of finding it. Now is when we need to revisit the working definition for truth we first saw in the **Foreword**:

Truth – requires that we *observe* facts and use *reason* and *caring* to discover what they *mean,* which we experiment with until we *acquire insight* and *create* **understanding.** Truth is **not** defined by what we feel, theorize, or intuit.

In confronting my parents, I not only discovered they did not love me, but they did not want to understand the truth about themselves or me. These were two facts I could observe by taking in what they said, what they failed to say, and seeing what both *meant.* For instance, if my parents had truly loved me, they would have felt concern that I did not *experience* being loved. Also, if they had wanted to see the truth, they would have asked questions so they could learn from the moment, not criticize and punish so all communication was effectively shut-down.

What people normally do is deny the facts, or if they acknowledge the facts they *explain* them away rather than observe what they *mean.* So I could have ignored my parent's actions and believed that just because they were my parents, they loved me. Or I could have acknowledged their actions, but then explained the *meaning* so I could *believe* I was loved, again, *just because they were my parents.* Or I could have done what I did and confronted them, but refused to accept what their reactions *meant* in terms of revealing the truth about the *differences* between their motivations and purposes and mine.

My choice was to observe the facts and their meanings, and then see whether my initial interpretations were confirmed by subsequent experiences. This process is one way I *double-check* myself, and expand my understanding.

What I learned from observing my parents over a lifetime is they never did care about love, truth, or beauty. Nor did they care about themselves, each other, my brother, or anyone else as far as I could see. One consequence is they both died alone, the only people present at the end of their lives were paid attendants. Their lives were defined by the same facts as any other mammal. They were born, mastered survival, mated, procreated, entertained, and fell off the cliff into the abyss with no internal fulfillment, consciousness, caring, or genuine emotional bonds.

To me, my parents experience was a frightening story of *facts, responses, and consequences* that provided a cautionary tale not to be ignored. I have seen this tale repeated over and over so often, I now consider it normal. What life has so generously taught me is that the only remedy for this normal internal tragedy is learning how to integrate love, truth, beauty and wisdom into everyday life.

My parents' lives were easy to observe and assess because they were extreme, and unbeknownst to them, even well-defined. On the one hand, they were salt of the earth — born and raised in Middle America (Detroit, Michigan), complete with a mid-western work ethic, and *family values*! On the other hand, they were totally self-absorbed, valued security above all else, (important to note — they died anyway) and never acknowledged a single internal responsibility or understood one internal need or potential.

In baseball terms, their lives were an internal no-hitter. Most people's lives are not so easy to observe and assess. Instead, most people learn to play the normal game well-enough to keep people around, sometimes, for a lifetime. Nonetheless, when all is said and done, most of us do not develop our minds and emotions, master love and wis-dom, and fill our lives with beauty and emotional bonds. As a result, in spite of receiving a sentimental or preten-tious eulogy, very few people have enough internal devel-opment to even want to integrate love, truth, and beauty into their daily lives.

In **_The Diary of Anne Frank_**, Anne talks about the issue of pursuing truth when as a thirteen year old girl in Nazi occupied Holland she "had thirty or so *friends*, but no one I can really talk to." She also had "the best parents in the world," but again she could not talk to them about real is-sues.

Two years after avoiding the Nazis by hiding in an at-tic, Anne confronted her father in a letter saying that she could not talk with him about real issues, and her Dad's response was similar to my parents, he was angry and hurt that she could say such a thing. While he did not punish her externally, he did punish her internally by being angry for a long time, and never asked her a single question. Like any person with normal training, he did not want the truth! Strangely, Anne learned the same lesson I did.

Anne's response was also similar to mine. She decided to continue pursuing truth, alone, and without support or guidance. By contrast, Anne's father lived and died self-absorbed and clueless—an unintentional emotional miser. A 'nice guy' who never gave what was needed. Anne gave the world her insight, innocence, courage and honesty.

What legacy would you prefer? The normal pretense of being a nice person when in fact you are clueless, or offer the world a conscious person who is committed to love, truth, and beauty? For me, it is another no-brainer choice.

A Helpful Guru

I chose to pursue truth starting at a young age. In elementary school (third and fourth grade), I started reading biographies of famous people specifically so I could see how they lived and died. I wanted to learn how famous people had responded to this mystery of being alive to see what I could learn to answer my question, "What, *if anything*, will make human life *internally* satisfying and meaningful."

I read approximately forty biographies between third and fourth grade and built an inventory of attitudes, purposes, and activities that provided insight into my question. One lesson I learned was that no one I read about consciously asked and answered my question. Some just didn't care and missed the point entirely. Others were successful in making their lives externally satisfying, but not internally meaningful, etc.

Thomas Jefferson, for example, was insanely brilliant and mastered many *external* pursuits that included surveying, farming, architecture, played violin, wrote over 18,000 letters, invented numerous machines, was a vegetarian, and oh yes, wrote the Declaration of Independence, built one of the best libraries in the colonies, and was President of the United States for two terms.

On the other hand, Thomas was *internally* contradictory in that he wrote one of the most eloquent defenses of liberty ever, while at the same time, personally enjoyed the services of over 200 slaves. He also had a sizeable ego to support, never did get his finances under control and died bankrupt, and had real difficulty with being personal. In other words, he was human. However, for me as a young person pursuing truth, he was a fount of information.

For one, he helped teach me the value of mastering many things. While I did not hope to master as many external activities as he did, I was determined to master as many as my time and intelligence allowed. Mastering significant life activities seemed to be a satisfying external purpose. So as a young man, I set about mastering listening to music, being in nature, car mechanics, carpentry, diet and exercise, surfing, running and wrestling, as well as explored history, politics, literature, philosophy, science, economics, psychology and religion.

Part of what I learned from reading about famous Americans was that I wanted to be a man of action *and* a man of letters. Most of the people I read about were either one or the other. The real key to my learning, however, was I had a *question* that focused my mind with a *conscious purpose.* This purpose helped to separate critical information from interesting details or trivial facts. It also created a place in my brain to file essential information.

Without questions to provide both focus and purpose, we can encounter the ultimate answers to human life, but they will simply slide off our minds like water off a duck.

The most glaring deficiency I discovered in studying famous Americans was the lack of internal development. It wasn't until my late thirties, after earning a Ph.D. in Psychology and having studied the Western disciplines that I moved on to explore Eastern ideas and practices. I was still on the trail of pursuing my primary question, and one guru who was especially helpful was the Shivapuri Baba.

The Shivapuri Baba led an unusual life. He was born in India into a family of gurus and spent ages 20-45 living alone in the jungle in order to achieve enlightenment. Then, he spent 40 years walking around the globe meeting and teaching ordinary and famous people alike. He lived to be 137 years old, and died in Nepal in January, 1963.

The Shivapuri Baba never wrote about himself or his teaching, but an Englishmen named John Bennett who first met the Shivapuri Baba when the Baba was 135, wrote a book called **Long Pilgrimage**. From this book, among other things, I got three questions: "Who am I? What is truth? Where is god?"

In my late thirties, I had finished my own long odyssey

to earn a Ph.D. and become a clinical psychologist. I had also finished with scouring Western philosophy, psychology, history, literature, science, and religion in my search for understanding how humans from Western civilization had responded to being alive. So now I explored Eastern thought and spiritual practice and began to seriously meditate with the purpose of making a relaxed, receptive, and aware state of mind my permanent and default state.

In the process of training my mind, I decided to meditate on the Shivapuri Baba's three questions. This I did until I settled on using the question "What is truth?" for a little experiment. Just for fun, I decided to integrate this question into my consciousness to see what might happen. So I began to meditate on *what is truth* and to continue repeating it no matter what else I was doing until eventually I integrated it well enough that both waking and sleeping, sometimes in the foreground and sometimes in the background, my mind was constantly asking this question.

I never tried to answer my question. I simply asked it over and over, not knowing where this practice would lead. Then, after about six months of constant repetition one night around 3:00AM, while dead asleep, I heard my mind say in a clear loud voice, "Life is truth!" and I woke up laughing. *In an instant, it was clear to me that observing and understanding ordinary experience was the path to all the truth that really matters.* Hence, **life is truth**.

This experience taught me many skills. One, I learned to keep my mind receptive and perpetually focused. Two,

I learned that a constant meditative state does not qualify as *enlightenment,* but it is necessary for anyone who wants to *live consciously and learn constantly.*

Three, I learned there is no mystical place where we become one with the universe and attain cosmic consciousness. Instead, we have an ordinary and democratic opportunity to work hard all our lives until we become consciously and whole-heartedly loving and wise.

The Integrity of Truth

"All truths are easy to understand once you discover them. The point is to discover them!" Galileo

It is easy to say that I love Galileo. In his day, Galileo was accused of being *arrogant* because he dared to suggest that the Catholic Church's view of science was primitive and simplistic. In particular, the view that planet Earth is the center of our solar system rather than a medium-sized star we call the sun. Galileo even wrote a play where he put the scientific views of the Pope in the mouth of a character he called, Simplicio!

To Galileo, (and me) it was just funny, but to the Pope it was disrespectful to the point of being heresy. It is both funny and tragic how predictable people become when they are determined to deny the truth. Anne Frank's father, the Pope, and my parents all spontaneously came up with the same criticism for the messenger of unpleasant truth, i.e., he/she was *disrespectful,* and of course, *arrogant*!

God love'em, but self-righteous folks are **so** predictable. On the other hand, so are people who pursue the truth. For instance, Anne Frank and Galileo are similar in they both continued to pursue the truth in spite of criticism and pain. In Galileo's case, he was eventually given lifetime house arrest but saved from torture and death under the condition he keep his mouth shut about the position of the sun and earth in the solar system.

Galileo quickly weighed his options and decided to keep his mouth shut. However, there was no prohibition against other kinds of scientific inquiry, so he pulled out an old model from under his bed and revisited some early work he had done concerning the wave action of water. In the ensuing years, he performed experiments and added information to our understanding of the physics of water in motion that we still use to this day. And what of the infamous self-righteous Pope? Well, he is dead and gone, his life a travesty, and no one can even remember his name.

There are many life lessons here, but one of the most important is that in the process of pursuing truth we create an *internal congruence,* or *personal integrity* that cannot be acquired any other way. So now you ask, "And what is the significance of being congruent and having integrity?" Good question. The significance of integrity is that it is the source of peace of mind and ultimate internal fulfillment. Other than that, integrity is not really significant at all.

This last sentence may sound flippant, and I guess it is, however, if you observe the prevailing attitudes of ordinary people in the United States, as well as our business and political institutions it is obvious that integrity, and therefore the pursuit of truth, is **not valued**. At least not so you could observe it in our everyday priorities and actions.

What you can observe is that as a culture we worship the twin gods of profit and progress. In the pursuit of profit and progress we have justified any and all degrees of deception, exploitation, ugliness, and destruction. This has been as individuals, and in our political and economic institutions. A few people who consciously pursue love, truth, and beauty have provided the only counterforce.

From the beginning of our experiment with freedom we created basic contradictions between the facts of reality and the stated purpose in the Declaration of Independence. The stated *intention* was to create freedom, but the *fact* is we allowed slavery, and also disenfranchised a large portion of citizens (women, African-Americans, Indians, etc.).

Of course, nothing is perfect. What was needed was to learn from our contradictions, but what we have done is try to hide our contradictions behind favorable images. The consequence of hiding our contradictions rather than learning from them is that we forever fail to change. Instead, we unconsciously repeat the contradictions of the previous generation and never create *cultural integrity*.

For instance, in failing to learn from the contradiction of slavery, we then repeated our prejudice, deception and cruelty with Native Americans, Asians, Mexicans, women, children, and anyone else we wanted to exploit or thought might stand in the way of *a white man's profit and progress.*

Pursuing truth creates integrity in both individuals and cultures. The opposite is also true. Pursuing profit and ignoring truth creates a lack of integrity for individuals and the culture, and with a lack of integrity we create internal tension, dissatisfaction, and perpetual anxiety that over time becomes irresolvable.

What we need is to first identify all the contradictions in ourselves and culture, and then pursue truth until we resolve each one. This process creates integrity and builds peace of mind, and over time, makes us loving and wise.

The Structure of Meaning

Love, truth, and beauty provide the structure, or skeleton upon which we build lasting value in everyday life, or in other words, *internal meaning.* The equation is simple:

Love + Truth + Beauty + Time = Internal Meaning

Pursuing truth opens the narrow gate to love and beauty. Without truth, love becomes an empty obligation, an intellectual idea or sentimental feeling, but contains no power to nurture. Without the power of truth, beauty is exploited for pleasure but is deprived of the innocent purpose that gives her existence an irreplaceable value in everyday life.

There are a thousand ways to run down our time and get through life without pursuing truth, expressing love, or experiencing beauty, but not one can provide lasting value, or in other words, real internal meaning.

Of course, there is no need to take my word for it, just observe experience and check the facts for yourself. First, you need to define love, truth, and beauty until you understand all three. Then, observe people in books, movies, and your everyday acquaintance to see if you can identify those lives that seem to be rich with meaning—not only for themselves, but also other people—and those that do not.

Do you see anyone whose life is rich with lasting value (meaning) who does **not** pursue truth, love, and beauty? One key to understand meaning is to observe the degree that people pursue or avoid truth, love, and beauty. The way to measure how much someone pursues these three activities is to observe his ordinary priorities and actions—not intellectual intentions or sentimental feelings.

For example, Thomas Jefferson did pursue love, truth, and beauty within a limited framework, and to the degree he sought all three his life had meaning, and to the degree he valued control of pain over pursuing truth he sacrificed peace of mind, internal fulfillment, and real meaning.

What was true for Thomas is also true for you and me. None of us is perfect, so we can *expect* to make mistakes, and Mother Nature, impartial force that she is conscientiously counts every mistake for us, like our bodies count calories, and sees to it we pay for each one. The Old Girl is quite reliable in this regard, and never misses a chance to exact her due.

The problem for you and me is that we are often ignorant of the rules and never notice we are making a mistake until Mother Nature punishes us, and we wonder, "Where in Hell did that come from?" I have some recent experience being blindsided by old Mama Nature and have ruefully emerged from the experience genuinely humbled, a little devastated, sad, and significantly wiser. In everyday life as in the law, unfortunately, *"ignorance is never an excuse."*

A Personal Story

At 32, I was a licensed marriage and family counselor, at 35 I had a Ph.D. in psychology, at 37 I was a licensed clinical psychologist, and by 43 I had a flourishing private practice and a tri-level, 4 bedroom, 3 bath house that one of my bachelor friends described as "...just right for *one* person." I was single, had no debt, and lived on a third of my income. Bottom line, I was bored to death!

What to do? Well, why not *throw out the baby with the bath water?* So, while visiting a friend who lived in the mountains of Southwestern Utah at 9,000 feet, I saw a cabin for sale. It was a solid cedar two bedroom cabin with a 2 ½ car 30 foot long garage and a storage shed on 1 ¼ acres of view property. All for the staggering sum of $82,000.00.

I signed the papers on the spot. This began a 19 year love affair with the mountains, nature, a magical cabin, a true cornucopia of animals and birds, and the challenge and risk that comes from living in a place that gets from 24-36 feet of snow every year, and you cannot drive in six months a year but must snowmobile in and out.

For the first six years that I owned the cabin, I worked three weeks a month in San Diego and spent 10 days at the cabin. Then, at age 49, I moved to the cabin full time and stayed until age 59. At 59, I returned to San Diego to make money, as well as to connect with people again, so I could teach the specific steps to internal development that I had discovered while being in the mountains. This is when Beverly made her appearance into my life.

Bev had spent seven years talking to a therapist who relied on my work and who I had supervised and trained. Bev had also attended a few three to six-hour workshops I offered from time to time in San Diego. One fall day she decided to attend a three-day retreat at the cabin, arrived a day early, came by for a little pre-retreat hike and dinner, and voila, we were off to the races!

We seemed to be a perfect match. We both seemed to love classical music, nature, pursuing truth, eating well and exercising, meaningful movies, personal conversation, conscious touch, photography, travel, etc. etc. There was, however, *a fly in the ointment*, I was 59 and she was 33. Even then, I characterized this difference as being "totally absurd."

When I tried to break-up soon after the first weekend we spent together, she clamored that she wanted to be with me because she had experienced many relationships, but no one to share life, truth, love, and beauty. She also did not think there would be someone with whom she could share these four things to the degree she could with me. I put up a bit of a fight, but in 20/20 hindsight can see that in essence, *I folded like a cheap card table.*

At this point in the story, many male readers may be nodding in sympathy, while many female readers may be looking disgusted. I understand both sides. In any case, **Bev said she wanted to pursue truth even if it meant being alone for the rest of her life.** This point was the *deal-closer.* I thought that if we shared a love of pursuing truth, then this love could transcend the age difference.

In fact, a shared love of pursuing truth and beauty can transcend any *superficial* difference, maybe even the *absurd difference* in our ages. Ultimately, however, I learned that Bev made her critical statement more to influence me, than as a fact about her. Even so, for a very long time we were happy, like two synchronous swimmers moving through everyday life in perfect harmony. God, that was a joy!

Then one day a little difference poked her unwelcome nose into our daily life. At the time it seemed significant, but not huge. For the first year and a half we had sex all the time, almost every day. This was something of a challenge for me since lonely mountain men don't have much opportunity for sex. Plus, I was 59 and she was 33, so we were at opposite ends of the libido continuum.

Nonetheless, I happily discovered that persistent use actually increases capacity, and I managed to keep up; however, I was **not** leading, just trying to stay abreast. Then, six months after being married, sex dropped off precipitously. When I asked Bev she did not agree she had done most of the initiating, and did not want to discuss it. Seems like a typical couple issue, and a small or even predictable difference of perception, right?

It would be except this was the first time we did not agree on reality. Secondly, we differed over a simple and obvious reality that I knew for a fact was unmistakably true. When I pushed the issue and tried to discuss it, Bev became defensive like I had never before seen her, and it became obvious it would be impossible to explore the issue from any angle.

When this kind of thing would happen in previous relationships I would not let it go, and sometimes, it meant the end of the relationship. With Bev there were no other conflicts, we were recently married and I was totally committed, so I made a conscious decision to let the issue go and just hope it would work itself out.

The *external* part did work itself out in that our sex life resumed, but the *internal* problem did not. The critical issue was never about sex, it was about *discussing differences and disappointments.* If I had pursued this internal issue it would have revealed the real problem, which was our difference in wanting to pursue truth. This difference is what eventually killed our relationship, even though it took another four years before enough differences accumulated for Bev to utter the fateful words, "I am no longer attracted to you."

Her tone was flat, and the emotion cold and indifferent, so with a few questions it was clear there was no recourse, and nothing to talk about. In fact, I gave her reasons to be disappointed — CMED was not a financial success, I was masterful on the mountain but in the city I felt lost, etc. — so in part, I empathized with her feelings. Since first making her fateful statement, Bev has not wanted to discuss a single internal issue. Nothing, zero discussion. Her only response has been to say she is afraid discussion will make her *crazy*, refusing to define what that means.

The reason I suspect her initial *selling phase* statement about wanting to pursue truth was insincere is because had it been true she might want to end our relationship, but she would also want to understand the reasons.

There are many *universal* lessons in this story. One lesson is that sharing a purpose to love truth and beauty is the most solid foundation for an emotional bond that exists. On the other hand, the inability to discuss *differences and disappointments* will cause conflict that over time can become so deep it can never be identified or healed.

One consequence of no discussion was that even the joy of our past was lost and became only an empty fantasy, because the shared purpose of wanting to pursue truth turned out to be a manipulative mirage in the service of an undefined purpose. In the end, because we could not talk, I was mired in a mystery I had no power to explore. One *universal* truth I see is that when a couple fails to make it their purpose to pursue truth, then over time, they will no longer have anything to say or share, and their connection will inevitably fade away and die.

This is in part what I believe happened with Bev and me. She only pretended to share a purpose to pursue truth, so from her perspective talking would make her feel bad, and there was nothing she wanted to see or understand.

This has been a long story, and my hope is that you will learn lessons from it. One lesson is that pursuing truth is a required response to a satisfying and meaningful experience of being alive. Another lesson is that no matter how hard we try to avoid them, we all make mistakes, experience loss, and go through painful experiences where we have zero control. So how do we need to respond?

A life-affirming response to life's pains, losses, and mistakes is to pursue truth and *learn from every experience*. When we respond by learning, no experience is wasted, and we emerge from every pain a little wiser, if not also a little sadder than we were before. If we try to "get past" our mistakes and losses we never learn from them, so these experiences are in essence, wasted.

Finally, in part because of my profession, the experience with Bev has been especially humiliating, so I can identify with Beethoven who was appalled that *of all people,* **he** was going deaf. Even so, the humiliation has taught me *humility*, and time has shown me that pain and humility are necessary to develop wisdom.

Also, the depth of my loss taught me the breadth of my caring, and helped me understand the experience of love. All in all, was it *good luck or bad luck?* Don't know, but I do know I was changed, and nothing was wasted.

Wedding Vows

I, *Paul Hatherley*, promise you, *Beverly P*, a noble life. A life made full with meaningful work, adventuresome play, passionate affection, and constant change.

I promise to challenge you to think until you find understanding, and to care until you feel like your heart will burst!

I promise to protect you with my consciousness and caring every moment I am alive, so you will always be safe to be honest about your hungers, and never alone without someone to see and understand you.

I promise to be honest about my hungers, and I will be responsible for my every pain, and never hold you accountable for my feelings or failures.

Years ago, I wrote a poem I called, <u>Invitation to Live</u>. While I did not know it then, I was writing to you! Today, you have responded to my invitation with a whole-hearted, "Yes!"

Now, I offer my poem to you, as an invitation and a promise, my promise of a real life filled with risk and adventure, work and play, joy and sorrow, truth and beauty.

PH—2005

Invitation to Live

Come with Me
And Together—Hand in Hand
We will Travel the Universe
Skipping across Beams of Light
Clear-Eyed and Curious
Sharing every Wonder
Nurturing every Need
All the while Innocently Chattering
Like two Squirrels in a Tree

PH—2005

Bev and I wanted the traditional vows, and we also wanted to say something that was personal and just for us, so in the wedding ceremony we did both. I am including my version of the vows because I think it might illuminate the internal needs and responsibilities we all need to understand and offer whenever we want to love anyone—mate, child, or friend.

Of course, a romantic relationship is always an uncertain enterprise because it depends on two people sharing purposes and priorities, and even if we do our part well, we cannot fulfill another person's role or responsibility. Also, circumstances and people change, so there is never any control, just the opportunity to care, grow, give and share, while vulnerably doing our best to love and learn.

Experiencing Beauty

Beauty provides the oxygen that keeps the fires of our internal lives burning. Without beauty, the energy necessary to love life and pursue truth quickly fades. In its place is born an enervating apathy, or instead, the frantic energy created by an insatiable greed for material wealth and pleasant distractions.

Experiencing beauty is the life's blood that keeps love and truth alive and meaningful. Eliminate beauty, and we make life a desert where survival may still be possible, but real living is dead and gone forever.

PH — 2010

These thoughts came to me in middle of the night and promoted themselves as a possible opening for this chapter, so I got up and wrote them down. I still can't think of anything better, so they will have to do. What is your response, do these words have meaning to you?

To me, these words are pregnant with meaning because all my life the *experience of beauty* has been a primary comfort in my *lonely pursuit of truth* — and the greatest source of energy and joy that feeds my desire to experience and express love. Naturally, the beauty that any particular person prefers is subjective, and though life's menu is varied, it is not unlimited. For me, the *external* sources of beauty that I have subjectively preferred have been found in nature, music, books, movies, birds and animals, photographs, and sometimes, every now and then, people.

Of course, truth is a reliable source of *internal* beauty. A truth succinctly expressed with innocence and honesty offers lasting value, and as a result, provides an intrinsic beauty. This is one reason that over the ages people have either memorized or written down stories, songs, poems and special quotations. Love too, is a source of beauty because in *expressing love* we transcend normal purposes and fulfill a small part of our internal potential to be conscious and caring, which is one way to make life meaningful.

The most satisfying and meaningful experience of beauty occurs when we combine *external sensual* fulfillment with an *internal desire* to learn and care. This is a conscious creation, where we learn to connect *sensual experience with truth and love*. By contrast, the least satisfying experience is created by normal priorities and occurs when we pervert the experience of beauty by exploiting her for the primary purpose of experiencing pleasure.

Now is a good time to remind ourselves of the working definition for beauty we first read in the **Foreword**:

<u>Beauty</u> — is experienced through the innocent expressions of truth and love, and the varied creations found in nature, books, music, movies, and art. Beauty is a fulfillment for our senses, ***never*** an assault, and beauty is always in harmony with truth and love, ***never*** in conflict.

Being aware of the *purpose* for experiencing beauty, and seeing the content necessary to create beauty, we can now move on to explore examples of actual experience to see what is needed to integrate beauty into our daily lives.

<u>Integrating Beauty—the Basics</u>

The first step to integrating beauty into daily life is to awaken a conscious hunger for it. Without being aware that we *need* beauty for inspiration, energy and meaning, we often think of beauty as being *nice*, and exploit her for pleasure. With a normal attitude, we passively wait for beauty to engage us. Typically, a beautiful sunset must serendipitously cross our path before we respond with a superficial but shrill comment to whoever is standing near, "Now, wasn't that just gorgeous?"

When we see that beauty is a critical *internal need* as important to our well-being as the *external need* for food, air and water, our attitude changes and we become active in our pursuit. We no longer accidentally stumble across moments of beauty, but instead learn about the sources of beauty and discover our preferences, so we can purposefully integrate the experience of beauty into everyday life.

Nature is a fine place to begin in our search for beauty because she is the source of everyone's existence, and one way or another always puts on the best show in town. When I started exploring the mountains by learning how to backpack, I also bought books on trees, flowers, birds and animals, so I could learn about nature's inhabitants.

A loving response requires we commit focused energy and interest and consciously explore and learn about whatever we intend to love. The process is the same in loving beauty—we must begin by learning.

In learning about nature, I began by learning every-one's name. Isn't it funny that the first thing we want to know about a new person is his name. Somehow, knowing someone's name makes him instantly feel more familiar. The same is true in Nature, learning the names of the trees, flowers, birds and animals helps to make us feel more at home in what is in fact our real home, but after a lifetime in the city often *feels* strange, and not at all *like home*.

If we read about nature, and spend time observing and being with her, then eventually, just like in getting to know a person, we learn more about the lives of trees, flowers, birds and animals until little by little we recapture our an-imal heritage and begin to feel as comfortable in our real home in nature, as we do in our artificial home in the city.

Do not panic, this does not mean that everyone who learns about nature becomes a tree-hugging environmen-talist who sells his home and moves to the mountains or desert. I am only suggesting we can learn how to be com-petent in more than one environment, and that being able to *absorb* and be *nurtured* by experiencing beauty in nature requires being consciously hungry, as well as purposefully acquiring specific skills and awareness.

It is important to know that just being exposed to beauty in nature does not mean we will also absorb and be truly nurtured by the experience. Too many times, I have exposed people to the very best nature has to offer only to see them be so self-absorbed and unaware that the expe-rience bounces off them with no observable benefit.

Absorbing and being nurtured by the experience of beauty, or truth and love for that matter, requires that we awaken to our instinctual and primal hunger for all three. Without a conscious hunger, no internal experience can be absorbed into our minds and emotions and nurture our well-being. This same process can be seen in relation to food for our bodies, which as you know can be unappealing to the point of repulsive after stuffing ourselves at Thanksgiving. Why, because we are not hungry.

Next, after becoming aware of our internal hungers, we need to learn how to experience beauty in nature, and this requires actively learning about the facts of nature, and how to take care of our needs while being in nature, because she is never concerned about our comfort or even survival, and will never be responsible for us.

Of course, we can walk in a local park or on the beach and never learn anything, but if we really want to make nature our friend and lifelong source of energy and inspiration, it requires an active and conscious participation. *Understanding this process is helpful in every arena of life because any experience we want to be satisfying and meaningful requires a conscious hunger, focused effort, accurate information, concrete skills, and enough practice that we become competent to the point of mastery.*

With mastery, we can spend time in nature—hikes, backpacks, camping, or staying in hotels while venturing out in the daytime—and we are able to observe, absorb, and be nurtured by all the life and beauty we find.

<u>Experiencing Beauty — The Practice</u>

My life-long love affair with *beauty-in-nature* began early. I spent the first eleven years of my life (1945-1956) in a small suburb of Detroit in a tiny two bedroom house at 157 Roth Blvd. The area surrounding my house was populated with dense woods and open fields where I wandered alone, found adventures, learned and loved, and through it all was perfectly safe.

It was here that I experienced the wonder of discovering a snake frozen in the ice of a small stream, chased frogs, found old deer antlers in the woods, and even came upon some farmers' wooden bee-hives. I both found and lost some innocence, for instance, when upon discovering the bee-hives I had to tip one over to see what happened. One lesson I learned was that sometimes it is impossible to be a little boy *and* pure-in-heart, both at the same time!

Other experiments also involved what seemed to me to be a loss of innocence. One happened when I was about 8, alone in the woods, and I decided to swear. My parents had sent me to a fundamentalist church and I thought God was always present, all-powerful, and would punish me for wrong-doing. Swearing was definitely wrong, so I decided to try it and see what happened.

I started small and said *Damn*, in a loud voice and to the empty woods. Nothing happened! So I escalated and said *Hell*, again in a loud voice so God could hear if he was listening and cared. Again, nothing. Finally, I said *Son of a*

Bitch, and still no bolt of lightning and no other observable sign from God. My entire vocabulary of swear words was now exhausted and I stopped swearing, but I did lose a little respect for God that day. In my mind, either He was not as powerful or all-knowing as people said, or He was a lot more lax about the rules than I was led to believe.

Funny how attitudes change, at the time of my experiment with swearing I saw myself on the *cutting edge of being a bad person*, and now, fifty-seven years later, it actually seems pretty innocent. My other experiences in nature were innocent, like discovering a wild raspberry bush in a field next to my house sporting three tiny green raspberries. I was so excited and patiently visited my little bush every day for several weeks until finally, they were ripe.

To this day, I can still remember the beauty of those perfect little raspberries, and the exquisite taste and texture of each one. Of course, with my fundamentalist training no experience would be complete without guilt, so I also felt selfish for not sharing my find with the family. At the time, it seemed I was doomed by a weak character that saddled me with *fatal flaws* to make me forever unlovable.

Ah, the joy and wonder of a punishing religion and indifferent parents. The only antidote was the beauty and innocence I experienced through loving nature, and in pursuing her even in these early days of feeling very small, alive, alone, and often lost in this overwhelmingly large and mysterious experience of being alive. To paraphrase Dickens, "it was a wonderful time, and a terrible time!"

At age 11, in September of 1956, my parents moved to San Diego and bought a house three blocks from the Pacific Ocean. I went from fields and woods to sage covered hills and pine forests; and from garden snakes, frogs, deer antlers, and wild berries to sandy beaches, wild waves, jack-rabbits, coyotes, foxes, and rattlesnakes. I was skeptical at first, but soon became happy with the change and quickly adapted to my new environment.

At the time we moved, San Diego was considered a small and sleepy distant suburb of Los Angeles that was barely out of frontier town status. The air was crystalline clear and the mountains to the east were etched into a shockingly blue sky creating a landscape that even my 11 year old mind found achingly beautiful.

I walked to school each day with my heart and mind ready to burst with the beauty of nature spectacularly displayed in an atmosphere that smelled sweet and looked fresh, and the whole scene was set in a serene beach town where a lone car would travel down the main street every five or ten minutes.

As you can easily imagine those days are gone forever, and I miss them. Now, everything is different. Right after a hard rain the air will be cleaner than usual, but it never has that heart wrenching, mind altering clarity it once had when I was a boy, and San Diego had fewer than a hundred thousand residents. The serenity too is long gone, as is the wonder of being able to walk on the beach after 7:00PM and be all alone. Now, no matter what time day or night there are always people on the beach, and the streets are never lonely.

In spite of my little experiences, I was still a city boy with a longing for life but not yet aware enough to know I needed extended periods of time in Nature. My *conscious* longing for beauty awakened slowly, as did my hunger to experience life through Nature. My early experiences in Detroit and San Diego were essential in preparing me to branch out in my early twenties and learn how to back-pack into the heart of nature, and listen to classical music.

Backpacking and car camping when we could drink from any free-flowing stream and never needed to secure a reservation to hike or camp was a far more serendipitous, adventuresome, and joyful experience than it is now. With fewer people, it was easier to be alone, and lonely. Back-packing in the Sierras, I had many an experience with bears, storms, lonely nights, and stark mountain peaks silently surrounding sparkling high country lakes.

I fell in love with stately incense cedars, and the robust reddish-barked Ponderosa pines. The Sequoias were far beyond my likes and dislikes, but left an indelible impression of ancient life. I also fancied Indian paintbrush, columbine, and wild iris, and I never met an animal or bird I didn't like.

For me, the most critical consequence of spending time in nature was that I could experience life and beauty directly and completely. My senses took in all the color, light, texture and sound that nature offers, while my mind grasped the reality of being alive with a newly palpable awareness, and my emotions responded with the whole-hearted energy of being inspired on the one hand, and terrified on the other!

The Need for Music

My first recollections of music were listening to 78 rpm records with Vaughn Monroe singing *Ghost Riders in the Sky* and Gene Autry singing *Gaffy – the Goofy Gobbler*. I was about 5 or 6, and even then I *consciously* responded to and still remember these songs sixty years later because of the *meaning* they conveyed.

Gaffy was a turkey who didn't eat much and stayed skinny. He was laughed at by all the other turkeys—that is, until Thanksgiving when Gaffy was the only one who didn't wind up on the dinner table! I loved that story. I identified with Gaffy, not because I didn't eat much, but because I felt alone in my priorities and purposes. Like Gaffy, even though no one else in my small circle valued what I did, I imagined that somehow the things I thought and cared about had an intrinsic value that someday, just might be recognized.

Another song I dearly loved was *Ghost Riders in the Sky*. Vaughn Monroe had a really deep voice and the song was about a cowboy who is given a warning to *change his ways* or he too, *will be chasing the Devil's herd across these endless skies*. Sounded good to me! I was intrigued by the descriptions. It began with *a lone cowpoke resting on a ridge* that saw the riders *coming up a cloudy draw* on horses *snorting fire.* They were *ridin' hard, their shirts all soaked with sweat.* The devil's cows *brands were still on fire,* their *horns shiny black,* and their *hooves were made of steel.* I loved that song, raw and real, and it was disturbing too, because it made heaven look dull and boring!

My life has been a search for lasting value, or in other words, *real meaning.* Nature and music are two activities that have provided a lifetime of primal beauty, adventure, and constant change. While some popular songs have provided snippets of insight and inspiration, it has been my experience with classical music that has provided a depth, breadth, and complexity similar to nature, which is one reason it has been a nearly infinite source of energy and inspiration.

When I began listening to classical music it seemed to be defined by *a lot of sound that went on for a long time.* I did not understand this music, and everything was unfamiliar. The instruments, orchestras, composers, conductors, the musical forms, everything about this music was large and confusing. What kept me pursuing classical music was the sound was organized and intelligent, filled with moments of love and longing, anger and laughter, joy and sorrow.

The sound of classical music did not give up her secrets as easily or quickly as *Ghost Riders* and *Gaffy,* but she promised to provide real meaning if I would only listen and learn. So I listened and learned over a long period of time, and the music fulfilled her promise and more. In return for learning about and loving her, classical music has provided lasting value in terms of warmth, comfort, companionship, energy and inspiration. All in all, she has been a very satisfying partner.

When I say classical music, I am referring to a relatively small circle of composers. The composers I listen to most are Bach, Hayden, Mozart, Beethoven and Vivaldi. Sometimes, I listen to particular works of other composers like Berlioz, Tchaikovsky, and Rimsky-Korsakov. Most of what I listen to is orchestral and is defined as a symphony, concerto, sonata, etc. These are my *subjective preferences* and have nothing to do with one kind of music being better than another.

Each person needs to explore the world of music to discover his/her own preferences. The point, however, is that our **preferences need to be based on a search for meaning, not pleasure**; that is, if we want the experience to be truly satisfying over time. This is a lesson for life, whatever we do primarily for pleasure will ultimately have no *meaning*. As a result, the *pleasure* we once experience will always fade, and often become the opposite—a painful emptiness.

On the other hand, any activity we pursue for the purpose of *meaning* will by definition provide *lasting value*, and paradoxically, the *pleasure* we experience from meaningful activities will increase with time. This is an important insight because beauty is *in the eye of the beholder*, so if we love meaning, then any activity that provides lasting value will be *beautiful* in our eyes.

My love for classical music and nature was completely fulfilled during the ten years I lived in the mountains at 9000 feet and experienced the weather, birds, animals, trees, water, risk and adventure all set in an atmosphere so clear that it made your heart ache.

Next, is a note I sent to Bev during the initial getting to know you *courtship phase* of our relationship. Here, I wrote as clear a description of my typical mountain morning as I could. Also, *Panda* is a wild kitten I rescued from the bottom of my woodpile after her mother abandoned her.

Hi: This morning was a classic mountain morning. It has rained cats and dogs for several days, but today dawned cold and clear. This morning I did weights and yoga, fed the animals, vacuumed the house, fixed morning drink and coffee, showered, and with chores done I sat down for music, coffee, fire, incense, Panda in my lap, and the most fantastic bird and animal show outside the window.

The music was Hayden at his best — harmonious as nature, beautiful as an October sunrise, as full and complete as the most primal hug and kiss you can imagine, playful as a kitten, and so satisfying that my chest aches with an experience that I love, but cannot keep.

On top of this, the fire is as cheerful and warm as the look in your eyes when we have hugged and kissed, and I know from your face that you are full inside, and yet, still long for more! The incense fills the room with a scent that is as subtly sweet as your warm breath, freshly washed hair, and flawless skin filling my senses, heart and mind with an indelible experience of innocent intimacy.

Looking out the window, I see the Magnificent Buck (the one with six point antlers), head to head with another buck about two-thirds his size. They go at it for about twenty minutes. The Big Guy won, of course, but no one was hurt and the spectacle was wonderful. At the same time, four turkeys were milling around interacting with six Fawns and five Does, while two of Panda's siblings were carefully sneaking out of their hiding place under the deck to eat the Kitty food. What joy!

As if this were not enough, I next went for a walk through Aspens so colorful that my eyes could hardly register their beauty. A feeling I sometimes experience looking at you! The air is crisp and cold, and I feel strong and rugged as I walk alone through the forest. Now, back at the cabin, it is time to focus my mind on *Building Bonded Relationships* (from *Life is a Mystery, Death is Forever, How to Respond*).

Perhaps, you can see from this little message there are some things that cannot be taught but we are all hungry to experience and share. What I am offering here is a glimpse into my mind and experience should you want to open this door and walk into a primal world of innocent beauty, sometimes shocking truth, and a constant love of just being alive. Talk to you later. PH.

One of the joys of living at 9000 feet is that the mornings are cold year round so a morning fire is always welcome. Since I fed the birds and animals, there was never a dull moment and the space around my cabin often looked like a petting zoo with many different species congregating and getting along just fine. The range of animals that dropped by to *Eat at Paul's* was wide and included bears, deer, wild turkeys, marmots, foxes, badgers, ringtails, squirrels, chipmunks, skunks, eagles, hawks and falcons, as well as about thirty different species of small birds.

I have to admit that I preferred the beautiful birds and the furry animals, but did not discriminate when the plain ones also dropped by for a free meal. Everyone was welcome and I experienced many adventures. For instance, the badger I approached too closely who hissed and lunged at me, and a bear who for months came every day for food and conversation.

Books & Movies

Reading came early for me and has always been a significant source of beauty, truth, and love. As a child in the third grade, I first read biographies of famous people, and then moved on to read every dog, horse, and adventure story that I could lay my hands on. I still remember many of them, but one set of stories that were particularly moving were the dog stories by Albert Payson Terhune. My favorite of all the dogs was a collie named Lad.

I loved Lad because of his beauty, but mostly I loved the intelligence, caring and courage in his character. Lad was Mr. Terhune's favorite as well. While I remember only a few of Lad's exploits, I remember nearly verbatim what the Master and Mistress said when they found that Lad had died sleeping in his favorite place under the piano. *Upon finding Lad under the piano the Master turned to the Mistress and said, "The train has stopped." but the Mistress, being wiser than he, said sadly, "No, the engineer has fled."*

I cried the first time I read that passage when I was about 9, and I'm tearing now. What these words meant to me was that two adults had the internal awareness to love Lad's character, and to share in the grief when he was gone. Also, while I could not have put it into words at the time, I loved that the Master was internally secure enough to acknowledge the greater sensitivity of the Mistress.

It was a complex experience. I too, grieved Lad's loss. I also grieved that I had no adult in my life aware enough to see into my character, and to love me for it.

While I never did find someone to see and love me, I did find lots of people and animals in books for me to love. I also pursued a profession where my job was to help people see their lives and characters without judgment, and develop their strengths and resolve their weakness. In essence, I made the study of character my life's work.

One person whose character was defined by loving truth and beauty was Anne Frank. At the tender age of 14, she wrote this innocent and insightful definition of love:

Love, what is love?...Love is understanding someone, caring for him, sharing his joys and sorrows....You've shared something,

given something away, and received something in return, wheth-
er or not you are married, whether or not you have a baby. Los-
ing your virtue doesn't matter, as long as you know that for as
long as you live you'll have someone at your side who under-
stands you, and who doesn't have to be shared with anyone else!

Think for a moment, how would you, right now, as an adult define love? Have you thought about love with this degree of detail? If not, what has prevented you? Does it seem that love is important enough to your happiness that you need to understand it in detail, so you can then master giving and receiving love innocently and honestly?

Where do you think the insight of this 14 year old girl came from? Let's look at the facts. First, she was curious and honest. Second, she had lost literally everything; her home, friends, freedom, school, etc. and she was cooped up in an attic for 2 ½ years with her life in constant danger.

Everyone else in the attic suffered from the same facts, except Anne was curious and honest, and she was the only one who *consciously* dealt with her losses. This meant that her hungers were etched in her mind and emotions standing out in high relief for her to read. It was from being aware of her hungers that she could define love. Without the inspiration of her circumstances she would eventually have come to the same understanding because of her innocent honesty, but it would have taken much longer.

How can we tell that Anne was aware of her hungers? She tells us about them:

About music Anne says:

There was a beautiful Mozart concert on the radio...I especially liked the Kleine Nachtmusik. I can hardly bear to listen in the kitchen (where the radio was located) since beautiful music stirs me to the very depths of my soul.

About missing her life Anne says:

Whenever someone comes in from the outside, with the wind in their clothes and the cold on their cheeks, I feel like burying my head under the blankets to keep from thinking, "When will we be allowed to breathe fresh air again?" I can't do that — on the contrary I have to hold my head up high and put a bold face on things, but the thoughts keep coming. Not just once, but over and over.

About having a purpose Anne says:

I can't imagine having to live like Mother and all the women who go about their work and are then forgotten. I need to have something besides a husband and children to devote myself to. I don't want to have lived in vain like most people. I want to be useful or bring enjoyment to all people...I want to go on living even after my death!

If you read Anne's diary you will see a young girl mature into a wise young woman. Her character is the central feature of her story. She is constantly pursuing truth, looking for beauty and trying to express love. In spite of feeling despair she sometimes has hope, and sometimes *continues on without hope.* She is brutally honest about herself, and everyone else too. Only a Nazi could fail to love her! She describes herself as *"I am not beautiful. I never was and I never will be."* Not true, she is beautiful in every way that truly matters: *consciousness, caring, and courage.*

I have gone into some detail about Anne to show that how widely we read or how long we live is less significant than how *consciously* and with *caring* we both read and live. Anne died before she was 16, and yet, in her diary we see an innocent girl who absorbed more love, truth, and beauty in her short life than any chronological adult with whom I have personally made an acquaintance.

When we read Anne's thoughts and experiences and look closely, we can see that a complex awareness goes into each sentence. If we read passively, skimming over the surface, most of the truth and beauty slides off our minds like burnt food off Teflon. This also happens when we react to life passively and superficially; that is, we miss all the depth and complexity, so experience slides off our unconscious minds and emotions without leaving behind any indelible impressions, lasting satisfaction, or real meaning.

Consequently, there is no point in reading a lot of books superficially, but we do need to read a few books deeply. In addition to books, we can also learn about love, truth, and beauty from movies. Movies can be lots of fun, but we need to work a little if we want to learn from them.

The point in choosing movies is the same as with books, we need to watch movies that add *meaning* to our lives, and anything that has *lasting value* will offer insight, and vicarious experience with love, truth, or beauty. The best movies, like the best books, contribute truly significant and memorable experiences in each category.

Does this mean that you can never watch a stupid

movie, or read a silly book? Of course not! No more than eating a healthy diet means you can never eat a cookie, indulge yourself with ice-cream, or in my case have a piece of pie. On the other hand, when you choose to watch a stupid movie or read a silly book, you never deceive yourself that you are doing more than giving your mind a rest, and you also pay attention to see if your mind is indeed rested by this activity, or even more drained because the experience is so meaningless. Is there ever any rest for the weary? Sure, when we are dead, we have eternity to rest! Just teasing—sort of.

One of my favorite movies is **Dangerous Beauty**. It is a true story of a courtesan and poet, Veronica Franco. She lived in Venice in the 16th century and was taught the *trade* by her mother because her father drank away her dowry, and there were few options for a young woman with a little rank and an abundance of intelligence, but no money.

Veronica meets and falls in love with Marco Venier, who is a senators' son and needs to marry for money and politics, not love. Veronica could have been Marco's mistress, but from a lack of dowry could not be his wife. Veronica had too much integrity to choose the mistress path, so instead became a courtesan, lured in part by the fact that wives were not allowed an education, but courtesans had full access to the library!

The story is about the life-long love between Marco and Veronica, and how Veronica becomes a well-known poetess, helps to save Venice from the Turks, and eventually is a victim of the inquisition. Every *external* part of this movie is exquisite, from the music to the costumes, settings, dialogue and story, but its real power is internal.

The *internal* relationship between Veronica and Marco is portrayed by intelligent dialogue and intense longing, pain, joy, integrity, and equality, all in agonizing detail. If you pay attention, you can learn about life, relationships, love, loss, courage and competence. In the end, you will love both Marco and Veronica, and dislike the hypocritical judgments of a self-righteous and sadistic religion.

In voice over's throughout the movie, the actress playing Veronica recites poetry the real Veronica wrote. I was intrigued and wanted to know more about this sixteenth century poet, so I researched her name and discovered that her poetry and letters are still in print. It was satisfying to learn what she thought and wrote, and how she lived.

Other movies that are also true stories and wonderful are **Cross Creek**, a true story of the writer Marjorie Rawlings, and **Miss Potter**, the true story of the author of the Peter Rabbit children's books.

Some great movies about teachers include **To Sir with Love** starring Sidney Poitier and **Good-by Mr. Chips** (1939 version) and **Music of the Heart**. Another meaningful movie that tells a true story rich in love, truth, and beauty is **Out of Africa**. There are many great movies that can teach and change us, but most movies are purposefully made to fulfill a mindless idea of what is *entertaining,* and as a result, shun *meaning* like it was an infectious disease.

The reason meaning is avoided is because people buy what they expect will be pleasantly distracting, and often avoid buying anything designed to make them think and care, and as a result, offer lasting value and be meaningful. This includes books, movies, and even conversations (which we do not usually have to purchase). So, if we want experiences from books and movies that will teach, change, and fulfill us, then we will have to work for it. I wish there was an easier way, but there isn't.

Until now we have been laying the internal foundation necessary to awaken a desire and open the door to creating a *meaningful* life built on the three pillars of love, truth, and beauty. How is it going? Do you see any differences between *normal* ideas about life and love and what you are learning in these pages? Or do you feel yourself becoming more curious about life, or experiencing a new longing to create something more meaningful?

If you are becoming curious and feel a nascent longing for something more in life, then you will want to continue reading as we explore what is needed to build a *conscious identity* based on love, truth, and beauty. We will also learn how to integrate the experience of love, truth, and beauty into every significant relationship.

Part II

Integrating

Love, Truth & Beauty

Paul Hatherley

Exploring Self, Life & Love

When you meet someone new what are the first things you notice? I have not done a study, but I think four characteristics everyone initially notices, consciously or not, are someone's *gender, age, race, and degree of attractiveness.* This is an instinctual reaction, and to some extent just common sense. People are complex, and when we meet someone new we have to start somewhere and we can determine gender, age, race, and degree of attractiveness without being obligated to say, or listen to a single word.

Next, if we decide from our initial impression that we want to talk with this new person, the next four things we want to know are his/her *name, primary activities, major beliefs, and recreational preferences.* Primary activities are defined in terms of whether or not someone goes to school, works in a profession, is retired, or nowadays, is unemployed. Major beliefs are defined by life-shaping values and attitudes, as well as religious or political beliefs, etc.

Throughout this *getting to know you* process, we gather information and make judgments. One judgment we often make quickly is the value we assign to a person. For instance, a normal American male viewing a Victoria's Secret model will probably have a one word mental response, *hot.* The subsequent judgment may be two words, *highly valuable;* and this can be in response to a lifeless poster without one word having passed between them.

Of course, American females are well-aware of this phenomenon, and it is one reason that being attractive is seen as so important. We all, male and female want to *feel desirable,* but we don't want to earn our value, we want it to be automatic, which is why we all want to be *hot.*

What I have mentioned so far are *external* characteristics. In observing someone new we also tend to note what we imagine are indicative of *internal* characteristics, like someone's demeanor—friendly or sullen, warm or cold—and does he/she seem genuine, make me laugh, or seem intelligent, kindly, relaxed, tense, etc.

It is important to notice that the process we use to acknowledge and evaluate new acquaintances is similar to the process we use to assess ourselves. The sum of internal and external characteristics that we observe, or imagine to be true about ourselves often creates a simplistic picture of the *complex structure of characteristics* we call *identity.*

Everyone's identity is built in childhood, when we see ourselves reflected through our parent's eyes. If our parents are warm and accepting, we tend to like ourselves. By contrast, if our parents are critical or indifferent, then we often seize upon any inadequacy, real or imagined, and over time *identify* with it. Our minds want to explain our parent's reaction, and the only option is to blame our parents or ourselves. This is often the last time we willingly *take the blame.* If we do blame ourselves, the reason is we cannot tolerate finding fault in parents we are dependent upon for our mental, emotional, and physical needs.

We all want our parents' approval more than anything, so if we are disapproved or criticized, we normally assume it is because we are not worthy, or *fatally flawed*, and so begins a very normal lifetime battle with self-worth.

Simple Self-Awareness

If you observe yourself objectively, similar to how you would view a new acquaintance, what do you see? Surely, you see your gender accurately, while *degree of attractiveness, race,* and *age* may contain confusing or painful issues. In fact, you may respond to each observation with emotions that range from neutral, to intense pride or pleasure, to fear and loathing. This is the beginning of seeing the complex structure that defines identity. Part of what makes identity complex is our *emotional reaction* to each real or imagined characteristic that describes who we are.

Where does the complex sequence of characteristics that form our identity come from? Good question. As we have seen, our first impressions are formed by how our parents see us, and then by ordinary events early in life that create an *image* of ourselves. This image may be conscious or not, and may accurately reflect reality, or not. The more our self-image is conscious and accurately reflects facts, the more connected to reality we will be, and the more our self-image is inaccurate or just unconscious, the more normal and neurotic we will be. It's actually a very simple equation that is sometimes accompanied by devastating consequences.

Degree of attractiveness, real or imagined, is always a significant characteristic in building self-awareness. It does not matter where we are on the continuum, attractiveness will be a significant issue. So if we are exceptionally attractive it will be an issue just the same as if we are exceptionally plain, and every place in-between. One reason is that we tend to rate our *value* in terms of how attractive we feel, or how attractive other people say we are.

When I was a child, my parents treated me as if they did not care about me, as I have already mentioned, by denying innocent activities and giving broken or useless gifts. They also communicated a lack of caring by never touching me. Even punishment was delivered with a belt.

One consequence was that I grew up believing that I was too repulsive for anyone to find me desirable, or want to touch me. This belief became particularly painful when as a teenager I wanted to have a girlfriend. Walt Whitman said somewhere that "any well-conditioned body is attractive" so I set about making my body well-conditioned.

I still felt that I was intrinsically undesirable, so I set out to make myself *internally* attractive. This meant I must be able to talk with a girl and structure activities so she had fun and felt satisfied. My parents' behaviors lead me to believe I was *fatally flawed* and *terminally undesirable.* My response was to become as externally attractive as I could, and then I worked on understanding other people in the hope that I could make up for my *external* shortcomings through what I was competent to offer *internally.*

As it turned out, feeling fatally flawed and terminally undesirable lead to improving my character, in part because I *responded* by wanting to understand other people. Growing up insecure in my value and feeling that I was the American equivalent of the Hunchback of Notre Dame was also damaging. For one, I developed a skewed self-image that did not fit the facts; and two, I made choices based on feeling that not only was I unattractive, but I could never be truly valuable to another person.

I mention my experience because a lack of self-worth is for many people often tied to a feeling of being unattractive, and as a result, creates a feeling they lack value as a person. Of course, feeling undesirable is a common source of low self-worth in children, and this feeling is rarely backed up by a single fact. In fact, most children who feel undesirable are in truth quite the opposite, but they often see themselves as being neither valuable nor desirable.

When low self-worth becomes part of a child's *identity*, it follows him into adulthood and often remains as a lifetime handicap that diminishes energy, reduces satisfaction in accomplishments, causes depression, and ruins relationships. What most of us do in reaction to low self-worth is to pursue approval hoping that if we get enough we will create lasting value in our own eyes. The only problem is this process can never work.

As adults, the only remedy to low self-worth is to develop the internal and external competence required to master needs and potentials: approval helps not a bit.

Facts vs. Feelings

The self-worth needed for a *conscious identity* must be built on facts, not feelings. In normal life we are trained to build self-worth on *feelings* of value, rather than the *fact* of becoming competent to feed needs and fulfill potentials. One consequence is that a *normal identity* is based on a superficial desire to *feel good,* and the two easiest paths are to be physically attractive, or to be professionally successful and acquire a large bank account.

Generally, men and women understand this principle, which is one reason men have traditionally pursued success and money, women have pursued attractiveness, and both genders have wanted the power of *feeling desirable.* One of the problems that arises is that even if we are successful in feeling desirable, we do not in *fact* feed our internal needs or create meaning, i.e., lasting value. Instead, even if we acquire success, money and physical attractiveness, we still spend our lives internally insecure and often discontent, but never know precisely what we are missing.

By contrast, if we build our identity on wanting to express love, pursue truth and experience beauty, then we build our core character on the solid pillars necessary to become loving and wise and create a meaningful life. One inevitable consequence of building our character on love, truth, and beauty is that we **master internal needs and potentials**, while also learning to love life and nurture other people. This is the heart of a **conscious identity**.

Self-Awareness & Core Character

Real self-awareness creates a *conscious* connection to the experience of being alive and alone in a mysterious and often impersonal world. Self-awareness is never a consequence of building an *image* of ourselves based on feelings and beliefs. Instead, an accurate self-awareness requires we learn how to *observe, think, learn, and change* — **not** sit on a virtual couch and believe, judge, and draw conclusions, or create sentimental feelings and mystical fantasies.

So look closely into the mirror, and ask, "Who am I?" Are you someone who has followed the normal program and pursued success, approval, security and pleasure? Or have you been a rebel and followed your own path, only to discover that rebels tend to be *against something* — and frequently fail to define precisely what they are for, and need to create? Or perhaps you have been a *reluctant conformer* who has seen there is something missing in normal life, but has never been able to pinpoint precisely what is missing, or on the positive side, see in detail what is needed?

Many people pursue personal growth through self-help books and seminars, as well as religious and/or spiritual beliefs and practices only to discover they have not mastered internal needs and potentials, and have not become *internally fulfilled people, satisfying mates, competent parents and real friends.*

The importance of seeing ourselves accurately is that we need to see precisely where we are now, have been in the past, and want to go in the future. This will help us see ourselves, identify our options, and create contrasts, which we need to grow and change. *It is a fact that our minds need contrast to understand anything. If we only see one side of an issue, then we cannot understand what is true, much less see our options and make conscious choices.*

In everyday life this means that understanding kindness requires we also define cruelty. To understand becoming conscious, we must see ignorance and oblivion. To understand internal fulfillment and meaning, we must observe the contrast provided by emptiness and futility. To understand change, we must observe the status quo.

To acquire understanding and make conscious choices requires we observe the *contrasting details* that define both sides of each reality. With normal training we adopt ideas, beliefs or judgments about life's significant issues, but never observe the specific *experiential details* necessary to first understand the options, and then make conscious choices.

Without a detailed awareness we never develop the power to grow, which often leads to a lifetime of wasted effort, anxiety, frustration, and a painful degree of futility. By contrast, when we learn how to integrate *expressing love, pursuing truth, and experiencing beauty* into our daily lives and core characters, then everything changes. Now, we have the power to fulfill our potential to create a satisfying and meaningful life that we always intuitively felt was needed, but could never clearly define, or teach ourselves, step by step, the necessary skills and awareness.

Experiencing Love

Can you define the experience of love? I am not referring to the attachment you feel for a favorite object, the desire you feel for a mate, the protective feelings you have for a child, or the dependency you feel toward a pet. Instead, I am talking about a *commitment to care* that is integrated into our characters, and is the core of a *conscious identity*.

The love I am referring to defines our basic *response* to the fact of being alive and alone in a mysterious, wonderful, and sometimes terrifying world. The love I am referring to is expressed in part by a commitment to *understand* every significant aspect of the complex experience we call life, with the purpose of applying this awareness toward *nurturing* ourselves, other people, and nature.

With normal training, love is defined in terms of our *feelings,* and often gets mixed up with contrary feelings: like fear, lust, greed, advantage, or a desire to control, to name a few. Defining love in terms of feelings is a slippery slope that makes it easy to slide into distortion, confusion, or perversion. On the other hand, defining love in terms of an *innocent desire to understand and nurture* limits our focus to observing facts and feeding real needs.

It is appealing to define love in terms of feelings because we are not accountable for actions, only sentiments. This means we can take credit for *feeling* like great lovers, when in *fact* we are self-absorbed with no awareness or skill to *internally* nurture anyone. Believing that we can combine *sentimental intentions* with the *fact of being inadequate* to feed a single internal need and still be *loving* is so common it is normal, which is one reason that understanding love is often confusing for adults and children alike.

If we define the experience of love in terms of what in *fact* we *understand* and *nurture*, rather than *sentimental intentions*, we can replace normal confusion with innocence and accountability. When we express our love in terms of nurturing actions, we integrate caring into the core of our character and use it as a foundation for building a *conscious identity competent* to feed needs and fulfill potentials.

Building a conscious identity requires that we observe the *experiential details* necessary to understand and nurture ourselves, other people and nature. Both understanding and nurturing are complex tasks that cannot be defined and mastered quickly or easily, which means we cannot reduce either one into a simplistic technique or quick conclusion to fit the normal *bottom line* mentality. Instead, the internal development necessary to understand and nurture must first be patiently defined, in detail and over time, and then we must practice until we master the required skills and awareness.

When we define love in terms of feelings it never crosses our minds that *expressing love* requires internal development. It changes everything when we see that real love is not defined by sentimental intentions, but requires a conscious nurturing of internal and external needs.

Truth Makes Love Real & Powerful

For anyone who wants to love life and other people — pursuing truth must become the central supporting pillar in building a conscious identity. With normal training our first priority is to control *security, success, entertainment, and feeling good about ourselves.* We are **not** taught how to make *pursuing truth* the core of our identity.

What we pursue everyday reveals what we care about, and defines our core identity and character. When we *pursue control,* we build a *normal identity and character,* so it is never our purpose to explore life's mysteries, to learn what is true, or to master internal needs and potentials.

By contrast, when we consciously *pursue truth,* our purpose is to explore life and understand its mystery and magic, as well as its pain. Since we see that controlling life is not possible, we don't try. Instead, we work on building a *conscious identity* based on pursuing truth, but where to begin? We start by observing everyday experience with the *purpose* of creating *detailed definitions* of internal needs and potentials that we consciously test for accuracy.

For instance, try asking yourself, "Who am I?" One answer to this question is that human beings are defined by the fact that we all possess a mind, body, emotions and lifespan. With normal training, we often take these four facts for granted, and then assume that we are defined by the level of success, security, and approval we achieve. When we question these normal assumptions and see that in fact we are defined by possessing a *mind, body, emotions and life-span,* then we re-define both life and ourselves to be in harmony with the facts of reality.

Now, we see that mastering physical needs is critical to doing what we can to protect the time allowed by lifespan. We also see that mastering our mental and emotional needs and potentials is required to build lasting happiness, and create real meaning. One result of acknowledging life's basic facts and fulfillments is that we want to move *away* from pursuing security, success and approval, and *toward* creating a vital and real experience of being alive.

Famous writers whose literary works have endured over time intuitively understand they need to experience life at its most real and primal before they can write stories that are timeless in value and meaning. As a young man, I read many stories by Mark Twain, Jack London, John Steinbeck, Stephen Crane and Zane Grey. I was touched, taught, and inspired by these stories, but I was also curious about the authors. I wanted to understand the choices they made and the lives they created so I could understand the experiential sources of their stories.

What I discovered was that each author chose to engage his life in as direct and primal a manner as possible. For authors like Stephen Crane and Jack London, the pursuit of life at its most primal created painful consequences. Stephen Crane, for instance, died when he was 28, and Jack London when he was 40. Both died young, in part because they pursued *external* life at its most raw, primal, and real.

On the other hand, Anne Frank and Emily Dickinson pursued *internal* life at its most primal and real. *The lesson for me was that I wanted to pursue internal and external life directly, and in ways that were intensely passionate and life-affirming, but not self-destructive.* I soon discovered that backpacking alone in the Sierras allowed me to engage life in nature directly and passionately, while also challenging my internal insecurities and fears.

In my mid-twenties, I found another way to explore self, life, and other people when a friend, Ken, stopped by my apartment in San Diego with his wife, Holly. Sitting on my bed, Ken said in a matter-of-fact tone, "Holly has cancer." Holly was 26, a year older than me, and was a stage actress. She had appeared frequently at the Circle Arts Theater in San Diego. Ken was a free-lance photographer, and they both now lived in San Francisco.

Holly had been diagnosed with Hodgkin's lymphoma. I was shocked to hear she was so sick, as well as by how nonchalantly Ken presented it. Ken and Holly had stopped in to see me on the way back from Tijuana where Holly was getting laetrile treatments. Before they left, I told Holly to feel free to stop by to talk, or we could go out to dinner if she felt like it on future trips to get treatment.

Surprisingly, at least to me, Holly acted on my offer and several weeks later called to see if we could spend a Saturday together. I said fine and structured a day with walks, a swim in the Mission Beach Plunge (Holly was a champion swimmer), and a drive. During this time, I heard Holly's story of her past life growing-up, with Ken, and now fighting cancer. She had my undivided attention.

Holly had a difficult life. Her father was an alcoholic who emotionally abused his family and mercilessly drove her to achieve. Ken was the photographer for the San Francisco Symphony, Opera, and the American Conservatory Theater. For contrast, he also provided portfolios for a large number hopeful young actresses and strippers. This last gig proved to be too much temptation, and one of their issues was that Ken indulged himself with the actresses and strippers.

When I took Holly back to her car, we were just sitting and talking and suddenly she grabbed hold of my face, turned it to her, and kissed me. Then, she said a little annoyed, "Do you always make the woman make the first move?" I was more than a little surprised and responded quite spontaneously, "Always, when they are married!" Thus, quite unexpectedly began a very strange affair.

After spending a few days with me, Holly called Ken while I was listening and her opening remark, with no preamble or pleasantries, was simply, "Ken, I love Paul." I had to admire her directness. Then, they spent the next two hours talking about it.

When all was said and done we agreed that I would go to San Francisco and help Holly through her radiation treatments. Ken was busy with photography and extracurricular liaisons, and a sick wife was a burden. I really liked and admired Holly and empathized with her isolation, loneliness and fear, and wanted to keep her company through this experience, no matter what the outcome.

The selfish part for taking on this responsibility was to learn about life first-hand. The meeting with Holly happened in June and I was just finishing a semester of five upper division philosophy classes. Holly rested in my apartment while I was taking the finals. For a week, my life was comprised totally of philosophy finals, doing my part-time job driving handicapped children to and from school, and spending time with Holly. All in all, it was a very full week.

After finals, I moved to San Francisco and the adventure began. Holly had a major role in a play called "Oh Calcutta" where she did a nude ballet with a handsome black man. Sometimes, Ken and I would sit in the audience together while Holly was on stage and the number of taboos I was involved in breaking, or witnessing being broken was quite staggering, as well as exciting.

On a more serious side, I was amazed that Holly never coughed during a performance in spite of the fact that she suffered from radiation sickness (a result of the cancer treatment) where a chronic cough and shortness of breath are inevitable and constant symptoms.

For six weeks my primary responsibility was to help Holly through a torturous experience. Five days a week we would make the trip by bus to Kaiser's cancer treatment center. After her treatment we would go to a deli to buy lunch, and then off to Golden Gate Park for a picnic.

We would talk and laugh and live as if all was well with Holly and the world.

Sometimes, we would talk about Holly's being ill and the possibility she would die. No subject was off limits. Mostly, we lived every moment like it was our last: fully conscious, receptive, present, and as innocent, playful and honest as we could be.

At night, I would break open myriads of vitamin E capsules and along with wheat germ oil spread it on Holly's skin where the radiation was burning her. The effect was to protect her from the intense burns all the other patients were experiencing. Even the doctors were amazed that her pale skin was so untouched by the large amount of radiation she was receiving, and they inquired about what she was doing.

My experiences were incredibly varied during this time. One day, while waiting for Holly, I sat across from a sad looking man who was getting treated for throat cancer. He lived alone in a hotel in downtown San Francisco. He cried quietly while he told me what it was like to face this illness all alone in the world, frightened, and with no hope for the future — whether he lived or died.

Back at the loft, where Ken and Holly lived, and Ken had his studio, I met many kinds of people. Ken served the cultural elite of the city, as well as some of the more sad and seedy characters. I, of course, noticed the similarities more than the differences.

One example was a black gynecologist and his wife.

Like Ken and Holly, and nearly everyone else at this time (at least it seemed like everyone), they were experimenting with "open" marriage. This intelligent and movie star handsome couple had the sweetest, smartest little boy I had ever met. At four, he had a vocabulary most college graduates would envy, and for anyone whose self-worth was secure enough not to be intimated, this little genius was an infinite source of innocent delight.

I also met actors, musicians, politicians, strippers, models, professors and aspiring young actresses. It was as they say, an eclectic group, and I listened to one and all and gathered information about human life, choices, and outcomes. It was part of my *identity* to want to learn. Everyone taught me: from the little genius to his parents, to Ken and Holly, to the sad man at the clinic. To most of them I was quite invisible, they were too taken with themselves to notice me.

Holly was a notable exception. She gave me too much credit. She tried to say that I saved her life, but the obvious truth was the doctors saved her, I just helped her feel loved and connected to life so she wanted to live, and in spite of the pain felt the struggle was worth the effort. And live she did. The radiation treatments were successful and in the fall I returned to San Diego and continued my *external* education *internally* touched, taught, and changed by experiences with real people struggling to find purpose, love, and meaning.

<u>Motivation & Purpose</u>

What do you think: can you look in the mirror and see yourself accurately? For instance, do you know in detail what *motivates* you? This awareness requires seeing what you *care about*, as well as every *purpose and priority*. Next, can you identify the *consequences* of your motivations and purposes in terms of the degree of satisfaction and meaning you create—versus the level of emptiness and futility?

If your training is normal, it is likely that your answers to these questions will be general, vague, and superficial. In normal life our motivations and purposes are an eclectic mix of intentions, assumptions, beliefs, feelings and facts that are often contradictory, and frequently disconnected from any observable reality. Generally, we tend to prefer confusion to clarity, in part because it allows us to hide from ourselves, and we hope—other people.

While confusion and contradiction are familiar hallmarks of a normal identity, a *conscious identity purposefully pursues clarity*. In developing a conscious identity, we soon see that clearly defining our motivations is critical to understanding our purposes and choices, which is necessary to identify *embarrassing contradictions* as well as create *life-affirming congruence*. A conscious identity requires we engage each life experience with focused attention, and learn from every event and person, no matter how painful.

Motivation and purpose are a basic *source of identity*— whether we become a writer, scientist, artist, teacher, a normal neurotic, or simply a warm-hearted and internally generous human being who other people respect, admire, and remember. Understanding our motivations and purposes is critical if we want to create a conscious identity.

As a young psychologist, (I was 35, which now seems young!) I wanted to be the common man's guru. What this meant is that I wanted to make an internally fulfilling and genuinely meaningful life available to everyone. This motivation and purpose came in part from growing up in a blue collar family where hard work, survival, and security were always the paramount issues, and internal fulfillment was considered a needless luxury, worthy of suspicion, and perhaps indicative of feeling *superior*, or *putting on airs*.

I still want to be the common man's guru, but it has turned out to be a bigger challenge than I first imagined. The problem that I did not anticipate has been that most people are not *motivated* to want life in all its wonder and terror, joy and sadness. Instead, people have taught me they prefer to protect the status quo, and often choose the *illusion of control* over the *fulfillment of love, truth, and beauty*.

When our motivations are normal, we want control, and information on internal development, while necessary to build a conscious identity and create a meaningful life, is not something we desire or value. Bottom line, *a burning desire to grow* is critical to all development. ***If we do not observe for ourselves that normal life is lacking, and that we want internal satisfaction and meaning badly enough to work and suffer for them, then information is useless.***

<u>Experiencing Beauty</u>

Everyone needs *warmth and tenderness,* but very few people can define these two words in terms of experience, and then use the information to nurture themselves and other people. If you want to test this statement, take a moment and see if you can define the experience of offering *warmth* in terms of *awareness, attitudes, and behaviors.* Next, do the same with the experience of *tenderness* using the same categories, and of course, all in *experiential detail.*

You may discover that precise definitions are difficult, even when defining something you think is obvious, or just believe you should understand. Let's try this together. For instance, to offer *warmth* we must be aware of our own *hunger for innocent attention delivered with whole-hearted energy and offered in a context of being understood and appreciated.* Once you are aware of being internally hungry, does it seem easy to imagine that if someone offered all the above, then you would define the experience as warm?

Considering the issue further; would the above definition suffice as a *working definition* for *offering* the experience of warmth? If so, does it make sense that if you offer this to your mate, children and friends, they will experience you as being emotionally warm? Of course, in some ways we have just begun to explore, because now we also have to define the words *innocent attention, whole-hearted energy, understanding and appreciation* before we can be competent to offer the experience of emotional warmth.

So now you wonder, "What in god's name does *defining emotional warmth* have to do with *experiencing beauty?*" Experiencing beauty through spending time in nature, listening to music, reading a book, viewing art, and sometimes just being in our own homes can fill us with energy and inspiration that feels *emotionally warm,* created in part by the pure delight we feel in being consciously alive.

If we are unaware of our hunger for a conscious life, we will not be nurtured by the experience of beauty. We must experience an *internal hunger* for the energy beauty can provide before our experience can be truly satisfying. Feeding a conscious hunger for beauty fills us with feelings of emotional warmth that are very similar to what we experience when another person offers innocent attention and focused energy in a context of acknowledgment and appreciation.

Living alone in the mountains of Southwestern Utah was instructive in teaching me about the internally nurturing benefits of integrating beauty into my daily life. There, I learned that listening to music every day, as well as giving my whole-hearted attention to the birds, animals, trees, sky, streams, and constantly changing weather filled me with deeply satisfying experiences of emotional warmth. These experiences not only eased the pain of loneliness, but also provided a daily dose of energy and inspiration.

There is another essential and timeless hunger that beauty nurtures. ***This is the universal hunger for a sensual and primal connection to the experience of being alive.***

Communing with birds, animals, trees, water, grass, and weather can all combine to create an innocent cornucopia of *sensual experiences* that have the power to fill a unique spot in our internal emptiness. By the same token, personal conversation with someone we love, and who loves us back, fills another unique space in our internal emptiness that can be fed in no other way.

The lesson here is that internal experiences are unique, and we cannot *control* them. On the other hand, we do have *influence* over our choices, and we need to use this influence to fill our lives with as much love, truth, and beauty as possible. To make this choice, we must observe that internal fulfillment leads to a meaningful life, while external gratification offers only a moment of stimulation.

It is also important to notice that experiencing and expressing love is always a beautiful experience when it is *innocently motivated*. At the same time, pursuing truth, also when innocently motivated, is another source of beauty that is within everyone's easy reach and does not require a partner! Instead, the beauty from both love and truth can be experienced and expressed all by ourselves alone, independent of anyone else.

The first step in everyone's internal development is to build a conscious identity based on self-awareness and the integration of love, truth, and beauty. The next step is learning how to create intimate relationships based on a sophisticated degree of other-awareness and the competence to feed internal needs.

Developing a
"Conscious" Identity

"I have a sense of self that is impossible for you to understand, and you will never possess." Moll Flanders, in the movie by the same name responding to two young women of equal age but superior fortune who were critical and condescending toward her.

Everyone develops an identity, but we rarely *consciously* choose who we want to be. Instead, we most often react *unconsciously* to parents, peers, and everyday life. Following this normal process we develop patterns of thinking, feeling, and behaving that become so integrated that we think of them as "just me." When our identity is formed by normal processes our *sense of self* is vague, poorly defined, and based primarily on unconscious beliefs and feelings that are rarely connected to the facts of reality.

This was the point Moll Flanders expressed to the two females who believed they were superior because they had more money and social standing. In stark contrast, Moll had developed a true *sense of self* based on first acknowledging all the brutal facts of life, and then responding by defining who she was, and who she wanted to be. As a result, Moll created a *conscious identity* based on working to understand life, needs, suffering and caring, while the other two superficial and aristocratically pampered females understood nothing about either themselves, or life.

This difference in mental and emotional development gave Moll a secure and genuine *internal value* the other two women could never understand, or possess.

We all need to develop a *conscious identity,* or *sense of self* because we need this awareness to fulfill our human potentials. If we observe the lives of animals and compare them to people, we see that in addition to a greater degree of *external* power to enhance or destroy our environment, we humans also possess an *internal* power to develop self-awareness that is not given to any other animal.

This means that no matter how hard an animal tries it can never develop the *sense of self* that Moll Flanders was referring to. All great writers, musicians, and artists create a *sense of self* that directs and guides their development. The rest of us must also complete this task if we want to develop a *conscious identity.* This is where expressing love, pursuing truth, and experiencing beauty become critical.

One consequence of integrating love, truth, and beauty into daily life is that we eventually *identify* with all three. The wonder in these activities is they develop our unique character like nothing else that life offers. If you doubt this is true, just observe all the normal identities around you perpetually seeking to control success, security, approval, and entertainment. What do you see happens to every-one's potential to create self-awareness, and with it long-term meaning, when his identity is formed around a com-pulsive desire to control life, while depending on enter-tainment to create a state of relatively perpetual oblivion?

What I see is that normal priorities make *expressing love* and *pursuing truth* impossible, while *beauty* is exploited for pleasure, and as a result, is not a real source of renewal.

The Structure of Identity

How would you define identity? Normally, we never even try to identify the *internal characteristics* that make us who we are. Instead, we accept vague judgments as "good enough." As long as our self-awareness remains foggy, we can *believe* we are masters of love, want to learn, are intuitive or spiritual, or whatever else our imagination desires, because we never *observe* in accurate detail the motivations and purposes that define our core characters.

In fact, the core of everyone's identity is defined and revealed by his motivations and purposes. As a result, normal identities are formed by *unconscious reactions* to fears and desires that are so universal, I call them normal. If we observe daily life, we see that we share strikingly similar *motivations* with other people based on *normal fears* we typically react to by creating *normal desires*.

Normal Fears & Desires

1. **Fear** of rejection, criticism, and loneliness.
   Desire for approval, because more than anything else we want to *feel good* about ourselves.
2. **Fear** of death, vulnerability, and being *out of control*.
   Desire to ignore the fact of lifespan, while also trying to control pleasure and security.

3. **Fear** of emotional pain, failure, and most changes. **Desire** for external success and to create a comfortable status quo; in part, by controlling feelings and defining reality in terms of beliefs rather than facts.

Normal fears and desires provide the source for creating our motivations and purposes. Look at your purposes, not the ones you *believe in*, but the ones you *act on* every day, and what do you see? Do you see that you too want to feel good about yourself — so approval, success, entertainment, hanging out with friends, and acquiring security are at the heart of your daily priorities and purposes?

If these pursuits define your purposes, there is no need to worry because there is nothing *wrong* with being *normal*. There are however, *consequences* of being normal, just like there are consequences for becoming conscious, or for that matter any other choice. It is a fact that with every choice, or even failing to make a choice, there are gains and losses. The trick is to define the predictable gains and losses inherent in each critical life option, determine what we prefer, and then make *conscious choices*.

Of course, consciously choosing the motivations and purposes that form our identities is critical to happiness. In normal life, we *unconsciously react* to normal fears and desires, as well as circumstances and genetic inheritance. When our identities are formed primarily from *unconscious reactions* it is impossible to see and absorb the information we need for internal development.

Gathering information to paint a picture of the identity we have already developed makes it possible for us to understand ourselves as we are now, and offers the option to understand and change our motivations and purposes, so over time, we can choose to develop a *conscious identity.*

Below is a chart showing the *internal structure* that creates a normal identity. It is important to remember that each individual adapts these *universal* processes in his or her *unique* style. By observing the source of our internal *fear*s, how we *react* by establishing *purposes,* and the inevitable *consequences,* we can understand our *normal identities* to a degree not previously possible.

Developing a *Normal* Identity

1. **Fear** of rejection, criticism, and loneliness.
    Purpose is to pursue approval for self-worth.
    Consequences — we never become *emotionally independent,* and proving our value is a lifetime project.

2. **Fear** of death, vulnerability, and being *out of control.*
    Purpose is to avoid unpleasant facts while trying to *control* feelings and outcomes. Judgments and beliefs are relied on as agents of control — while entertainment becomes a critically important distraction.
    Consequences are that *self-image* and view of reality are based on primitive beliefs and feelings, rather than observations and reason, so it is impossible to build self-worth or become internally competent.

3. **Fear** of emotional pain, failure, and most changes.

Purpose is to pursue success, protect the status quo, and avoid internal hungers and responsibilities.
Consequences are to become terminally dissatisfied because no matter how *externally* rich we become, we are forever *internally* deprived. Also, fear of change along with a perpetual lack of self-worth makes internal growth impossible, so a *meaningful* life is forever beyond our developmental capacity.

The best way to approach this information is to look for *grains of truth* in each process, rather than a *perfect fit* for your unique circumstances. This way you will observe the invisible processes that form the patterns of feeling, thinking, and behaving that form your identity.

It is important to not expect total comprehension of the information in the chart, or an immediate ability to change. Learning requires that we first expose our minds to new information, and then compare and contrast what we have learned to what we observe is true in order to confirm, modify, or dismiss the new information. Following this process, new information may *begin* as someone else's idea, observation, or discovery, but *ends-up* being integrated into our own experience and understanding.

Of course, the information in the chart is not all that goes into forming a normal identity. It does, however, identify critical elements that determine whether we create a satisfying life defined by self-worth and real meaning, or an unfulfilled life defined by a chronic lack of self-worth, and a gnawing sense of emptiness and lack of meaning.

The next step in creating options is to offer a different model for forming our identities. The model below defines a *conscious identity*. Here, the word *conscious* means that we *choose* this identity by *purposefully responding* to life's options, rather than *unconsciously reacting* to feelings. **You will note that in defining the process necessary to develop a conscious identity, the first and most fundamental step in each process was changed from fear to desire.**

Developing a Conscious Identity

1. **Desire** for self-worth and emotional independence.
    Purpose is to *understand* internal needs and potentials so we can *nurture* ourselves and other people.
    Consequences are we develop permanent self-worth, and create a satisfying life for ourselves and intimacy with other people. We also clearly define internal potentials and fulfill them.

2. **Desire** to acknowledge facts of life beginning with the fact that every life ends in death, being vulnerable is unavoidable, and no mortal ever has control.
    Purpose is to *understand* the *meaning* of every fact and become competent to respond effectively to every real need, surprising event, and unexpected feeling.
    Consequences are that we learn to see life accurately, become competent to feed every need, and generally, are relaxed with the mystery of being alive.

3. **Desire** is to learn from emotional pain and failure, and want to be competent to deal with the fact that life and change are *synonymous* and cannot be controlled.

Purpose is to use every experience — painful, joyful, or neutral — to unravel the secrets behind the mystery of being alive and to discover both *universal* and *unique* truths necessary to create satisfaction and meaning. **Consequences** are that we create an internally rich life characterized by permanent self-worth, consciously chosen purposes, real love, an innocent appreciation of beauty, and a passion for living that creates a degree of internal satisfaction and meaning that heretofore was not considered possible.

Controlling Negatives vs. Mastering Positives

Go back and review the chart for developing a *normal identity* and note that the first element is *fear,* while the first element for developing a *conscious identity* is *desire.* Also, note that we form *purposes* in reaction to the first element. When the first element is fear, then our purpose is to *avoid and control* rather than become competent. ***This is how we build normal identities; that is, we form our purposes based on controlling negatives and assume that if we avoid pain and loss, then the positive will just happen.***

By contrast, the basis for developing a conscious identity is *desire.* One consequence is that we are motivated to *master the positive* of understanding and nurturing, rather than *control the negative* of pain and loss. ***In developing a conscious identity we purposefully pursue a meaningful life by mastering each skill and awareness necessary to achieve our goals.*** This fundamental difference in motivation and purpose changes everything.

To begin, in normal life almost everyone fears criticism, rejection, and loneliness, and learns to rely on approval and fitting-in as a way to *control the negative* of emotional pain. The hope is that if we get enough approval we will like ourselves, and feel valuable. The only problem is that even if we succeed in getting barrels of approval, we still fail to become competent to master our internal needs and potentials, and so in both the short and long-term we fail to develop real self-worth, or enduring internal value.

On the other hand, if we begin with a *desire* to build self-worth, we see that mastering internal needs and potentials will create the *competence* necessary to establish and confirm a lasting internal value. Now, basing our self-worth on being competent to understand and nurture ourselves and other people, our value is built on *objective* skills and awareness, and one happy consequence is we become internally fulfilled and emotionally independent.

Take a moment and think about the people you know, including yourself, and ask, "How many people in my circle of family and friends have mastered the awareness and skills necessary to feed their internal needs?" By contrast, "How many people do I see are dependent on approval, so their self-worth is often in question, and a real concern?" My guess is that if you observe the people around you well-enough to answer these questions, you will see that approval is high on everyone's priority list. You may also see that few people can define self-worth, much less identify the precise skills and awareness required to create it.

After self-worth, the next critical issue in everyone's life is *personal fulfillment*. With a normal identity we fail to define the requirements for personal fulfillment, and instead, try to *control* pain and pleasure so if at all possible we avoid the one, and wallow in the other. Believing in and pursuing the *illusion* we can *control* life's pain, pleasure and outcomes is central to sustaining a *normal identity*. If you doubt this insight, then once again observe yourself and other people until you can identify everyone's fears and purposes.

For instance, in listening to everyday conversation does it seem that people value being innocent and vulnerable, and as a result, want to talk about, share, and explore their fears, longings, desires, successes and failures? Also, does it seem that people use conversation to pursue truth and develop understanding until they become internally competent to nurture themselves and other people?

Or does it seem that people keep their conversations safe and superficial, usually trying to portray the *best image* of themselves, rather than being honest and authentic? In addition, does it seem that people talk more about *external* success, along with their material things, travel and comfort, versus *internal* needs, purposes, love, truth, beauty, and the experience of meaning?

Also observe your own mind and see what you think about most. Do you think about *external* problems, success, failure, trips and purchases, or the *internal* issues of understanding, caring, consciousness, needs, purposes and how to create an *internally* fulfilled and meaningful life? What do you see are the *consequences* for the topics you choose to think about in the privacy of your own mind?

If your thoughts and conversations are focused on external tasks, problems and issues, then you will have little time or energy for exploring internal needs and potentials. This is what happens to most people, and is the reason that internal fulfillment and meaning are so rare—we fail to make it our purpose to explore and discover what we must understand to master internal needs and potentials.

Absorbing Experience

Developing a *conscious identity* requires we have some *consciousness* to build on! One problem with a normal identity is that we are taught to define reality in terms of ideas we acquire, beliefs we adopt, or sentimental feelings rather than accurate observations, rational thought, and real understanding. *One consequence is that with normal training, we frequently fail to understand even simple words when they describe actual experience.*

The result is that if someone talks innocently and vulnerably about daily life, pain, needs, death, purpose, or expressing love, pursuing truth, and experiencing beauty, it may create an uncomfortable and awkward silence. On the other hand, if we discuss ideas, feelings or beliefs, right and wrong, good and bad, then everybody has an opinion that he or she is usually all too eager to express. Strangely, it is easier to talk about the fantasy that in a past life we were Cleopatra or Alexander the Great, rather than how to feed internal needs or create meaning in everyday life.

The reason it is easier to discuss fantasies than real life is that a normal identity is trained to rely on fantasies, beliefs, and feelings as a method for *controlling* awareness of negative feelings and facts. So talking about feelings and fantasies offers a greater *image of control* than acknowledging that life is always uncertain, and never comes with an owner's manual, or that internal fulfillment is complex and that emotional bonds are largely beyond everyone's training and developmental capacity.

As complex as real life can be and feel, we all need to develop a detailed awareness of the daily experience of just being alive. Don't get nervous, I am not going to suggest you sell everything and move to a cave in the Himalayas and contemplate your navel 24/7. First of all, with a normal identity that meditative experience would not expand your awareness but constrict and narrow your world view even more! So save your money, stay home, eat well and take showers, and learn how to *absorb* the ordinary experiences you have every day, *think* about them in detail, and *learn* about life, yourself, and other people.

Following this formula will develop self-awareness, as well as awareness of what life offers. You will also learn about other people. For instance, you will see how people *unconsciously react* to internal needs and potentials, and how they have no clue how to *consciously respond* to what everyone knows is a frightening mystery that we call *life*.

You may wonder, "How does one absorb experience?" Great question. First, learn how to *concentrate and pay close attention*. This means that you approach every experience, even if it is routine, predicable, and repetitive, with the purpose of observing it like was the very first time. As a result, you drop all expectations, beliefs and ideas that constrict your awareness. You also focus on *observing* with your eyes, *listening* with your ears, and being receptive to *touch, smell*, and even *taste* if appropriate and it adds to your ability to gather objective information that you take in *uncritically* and *vulnerably*.

With a normal identity we look for something to criticize in every new situation, in part, because when we are *evaluating* we feel special, powerful, and important. Is there anyone who does **not** want to feel special, powerful, and important? The only problem with being masterful at evaluating and criticizing is we become *blind* to the facts and sometimes *deaf*, but not nearly often enough *dumb*.

If everyone learned to absorb each significant event or experience, he/she would be prepared to *think* about it. The purpose of thinking is to find meaning. For instance, the movie **Dangerous Beauty** is one that I deeply enjoyed and found to be unusually meaningful. I could be like most people and offer a superficial reason for my positive response, so I might say, "I'm a sucker for Catherine McCormick, and I like romantic stories about real people."

Or I could think about my response and say: "The lead characters, Veronica and Marco, were equal in intelligence, caring and playfulness, and their dialogue delightfully revealed that equality. They were also equal in their willingness to work and suffer for love and integrity. This movie tells a true story and part of its significance is that I have wanted to be in a relationship with a woman who could stand alone and be confident in her own intelligence, caring, and playfulness, as well as offer a whole-hearted willingness to work and suffer for love and integrity."

In the example of the first superficial normal response, I said nothing significant about the movie, or myself. All too often this is all anyone says, or thinks, and one consequence is that we often talk a lot, but say very little.

For contrast, in the conscious response I say something *significant* about the movie, and *revealing* about myself. The conscious response requires work, but has meaning, and is something I can learn from, and so can the person I share it with. The normal response has no information or meaning for anyone, and so slips anonymously into the black hole of normal conversations that are repeated over and over with no originality, authenticity, or meaning.

Tragically, what is true for everyday conversation is also true for the thoughts in our minds. So if our conversations are banal, safe and superficial, it is a near certainty that our thoughts will follow suit, even if we *believe* we are terribly profound. It is a sad fact I have discovered over a lifetime of listening to people that nearly everyone *believes* he is more profound in thought than in conversation, but I have discovered this is in fact, **not** true.

Instead, I have found that everyone's thoughts, and even more sadly everyone's *lives,* are revealed by the topics and depth of their conversations. If you want to assess the content, purpose and meaning in your life and thought, listen to what you say, over time, and the reality will soon be revealed. There is tremendous power in conversation that we are rarely trained to see or understand.

Once we *observe* and *think about* a meaningful topic, the next two steps are to *learn and change.* In the example of the movie about Marco and Veronica, one thing I learned was to separate sarcasm from playfulness.

What I could see from watching Marco in dialogue with Veronica was that he could tease in a playful manner that was satisfying for them both, and she in turn could do the same. In observing myself, I saw that sometimes with Bev, I would tease in a sarcastic manner that might have seemed fun for me, but not for her. Instead, by paying attention I could see sarcasm hurt her feelings, and was anything but fun for her, and in fact, not for me either.

Another thing I learned by thinking about the issue in more detail was that my use of sarcasm was often habitual, and seemed natural, while being innocently playful required more originality and thought. In other words, true playfulness was more work. What I was *learning* made it clear that I needed to make some *changes,* which I did.

One unexpected consequence of paying attention to my conversation and learning to substitute a *mutual playfulness for solitary sarcasm* was that together we developed a way to play with words and phrases. What happened was that we started with little cliché contests where we would banter back and forth to see who could most ridicule the normal use of tired old sayings in place of saying something authentic and original. Over time, we evolved into mimicking a backwoods Southern drawl into our banter as an added tool for having fun with our game. Eventually, we became fairly entertaining, at least for ourselves!

This is a simple example of how to use ordinary experience to *absorb, think, learn and change* in order to expand consciousness and make improvements to everyday life.

Building a Conscious Identity

The primary task is to master every skill and awareness necessary to replace an *unconsciously* formed *normal* identity with a *purposefully* chosen *conscious identity.* Sadly, completing this task is neither quick nor easy, and it is not something that will happen serendipitously or by osmosis. Instead, if we want to develop a *conscious identity,* then it will be step by step and layer by layer, over time. This complex process requires desire, commitment and practice. At least no one can say I am sugar coating this task in order to sell it.

Building a conscious identity begins with comparing and contrasting a normal vs. conscious identity. So study the two charts and notice the critical element at the base of each process. As we already noted, each process in building a normal identity is based on fear, while a conscious identity is formed from desire. Contrast the two until you *want* to trade in your old *fear-based normal identity* in order to acquire a brand new *desire-based conscious identity.* This step is critical to all real development.

Next, compare and contrast the *purposes and consequences* of both identities in detail. Understanding every element in both identities is necessary to identify *what* to change. This information is also necessary to observe the life-affirming benefits of a conscious identity, which in turn, are essential to developing a genuine *desire* to grow. Once you see what needs changing, and have developed a whole-hearted desire, then you are prepared to tackle the issue of *how* to grow.

Internal growth requires that we drop the attitude of wanting to *control negatives* and replace it with a *conscious attitude* of wanting to *master positives.* This change requires that we focus on mastering internal fulfillment rather than paying attention only when we have a problem to solve, or a pain to avoid. When our top priority is to master internal fulfillment—then learning how to express love, pursue truth, and experience beauty becomes critically important.

While love, truth, and beauty are essential for internal fulfillment and meaning, they do not even enter our minds when our purpose is to *control pain.* So as we have seen, the first step is to shift our ***purpose from controlling negatives to mastering positives*** After we change this purpose, we must actually master expressing love, pursuing truth, and experiencing beauty.

This is the truly fun part. It is also a lifetime task that allows our minds and emotions to expand every moment we are alive. Now, it would be helpful to re-read the first three chapters with a new attitude and purpose. Your mind needs to re-read *consciously* looking for critical topics to explore, skills to master, and insights that you can use to build understanding.

For instance, in reading the title of this book did you notice that love, truth, and beauty were expressed as *activities to master,* rather than *concepts or ideas to play with*? This insight is critical because when love, truth, and beauty are integrated thru competent actions they have the power to feed needs, fulfill potentials, and create meaning. As concepts, they are powerless to feed or fulfill anything, except maybe our egos and fantasies!

Another significance of the book's title is that it answers my life-long question, "What, if anything, will make human life meaningful?" I now see that *anyone who integrates expressing love, pursuing truth, experiencing beauty and developing wisdom* into everyday life will create *internal meaning*. This realization did not surprise me like the exciting cork popping, champagne gulping epiphany I had expected, but instead, slowly seeped into my brain over the past few weeks since I changed the title to what it is now.

What I see is that when love, truth, and beauty are precisely defined actions, then we can learn the objective skills and awareness that allow us to apply all three activities in a nearly infinite number of ways. This means that expressing love, pursuing truth, experiencing beauty and developing wisdom can be learned and taught like language or mathematics, and this will enable each person to fulfill his/her unique potentials. The only fly in the ointment is we have to commit to working and learning.

Bottom line, there is no substitute for kicking our coach potato minds off the virtual lazy boy recliner and onto the running track of real life. When someone wants to work there is no preventing his growth and internal development. This means that if anyone creates a conscious purpose to master love, truth, beauty and wisdom backed-up by genuine desire and the information from my books, he can master internal needs and potentials.

In the end life is a mystery, death is forever, and all that matters is how we respond. If our response is *normal,* then we pursue success, security, and entertainment; and if *conscious,* we integrate love, truth, and beauty. Your choice!

Paul Hatherley

Building Emotional Bonds

Life is often lonely, and throughout history people have reacted to loneliness by trying to build emotional bonds. In songs, poems, movies and novels, as well as books on psychology and self-help, we read countless stories and are given endless advice for how to pursue *love*, but no information about how to express and maintain love after we find it! Sometimes, we find love only to lose it, and sometimes, we spend our entire lifetime longing for emotional bonds that never quite materialize.

Part of the problem is that in stories where love seems to be real and promises to last, the most we are told is "...they lived happily ever after." This is never enough information to learn how to build an emotional bond, or how to express and maintain it for a life-time. Instead, we learn from personal experience, movies, books, and self-help about love's allure, pitfalls and tragedies, but do **not** learn how to *create and maintain* genuine emotional bonds with our mates, parents, children, or friends.

One problem is that emotional bonds can never replace the satisfaction and meaning we need to create all alone in our individual lives. This means that a conscious identity is required to first create internal fulfillment for ourselves, so we are internally prepared to build an emotional bond with another person. Bottom line: *No internal development or conscious identity for ourselves – no emotional bonding.*

<u>Loneliness vs. Emptiness</u>

One *principle of life* that is perpetually useful states that *purpose determines outcome.* This means that when our purposes are *congruent* with our needs and potentials, then our lives will be satisfying. On the other hand, if our purposes *conflict* with our needs and potentials, then the *outcome*, i.e. our experience of life, will be unsatisfying.

Applying this principle to emotional bonding, we see that if first we become *competent* to feed our internal needs, and then *consciously* respond to loneliness by fulfilling our potential to *give, grow and share*, then we will create a truly satisfying outcome — a genuine emotional bond — assuming we find someone who is similarly inclined and developed.

If instead, we are **not** competent to feed internal needs, and *combine* loneliness with neediness so our purpose is to get a relationship to fulfill both, then the *outcome* can never be satisfying or meaningful. Now is a good time to ask, "What have I wanted from intimate relationships, and what have I offered." For instance, have you fed your *internal* needs and become *emotionally independent*, or do you lean toward being internally needy and dependent?

The critical point here is that in acquiring mental and emotional development we inevitably learn how to build emotional bonds, but if we remain internally *un-developed*, then we never acquire the necessary awareness and skill. Surprisingly, this insight reveals that the ultimate source for building emotional bonds is *internal development*.

Pursuing Truth

At the heart of every emotional bond is sharing, and becoming competent to see and share the *truth* in everyday life is the most powerful glue we have in both forming and maintaining emotional bonds. In normal life, the most we usually share are *feelings and fantasies*. From this fragile foundation we may *imagine* an emotional bond exists, but in *fact* this bond proves to be weak as conflict, pain, time and reality quickly erodes and eventually breaks a normal relationship based on illusions and superficial sentiments.

Perhaps you can see a thread running through internal development: that is, **actively pursuing truth is the core of a conscious identity and the heart of an emotional bond.** It is important to also note that we can *pursue* truth, and sometimes *see and understand* the critical facts and needs, but we can never *possess* the truth. The truth is never ours, she belongs to herself, stands alone, and never cares a whit about what we believe, feel, fear, or desire.

If you remember, **life is truth**, and together life and truth are always in motion, never static, and never under anyone's control. Our job as human beings is to learn how to observe, absorb, learn from, and share both life and truth. Growing and sharing are necessary for intimacy, so it is important that everyone master pursuing and sharing truth to discover for himself whether or not this provides a basis for building a genuine emotional bond.

<u>Warmth & Tenderness</u>

We first brought up warmth and tenderness in relation to experiencing beauty. It is a key issue here because we all need the experience of warmth and tenderness in our important relationships, but in being busy we often fail to make the time, or consciously learn how to offer these two basic elements necessary for emotional bonding.

Earlier, we defined emotional warmth as requiring ***innocent attention delivered with whole-hearted energy and offered in a context of acknowledgment and appreciation.*** In the initial courtship, or selling phase of a romantic relationship most of us at least try to provide warm attention and focused energy. The reason is we want to make a *good impression* and often realize intuitively, if not consciously, that giving attention is needed if we want to be liked.

After a successful *selling phase*, we encounter the task of how to express and expand our new romance. This is when we run into difficulty. Now it becomes important to master giving innocent interest and focused attention, and in the process develop the skills necessary to understand the experience of someone we think we already *know*.

It is much easier to explore the experience of someone we obviously do **not** know than someone who is familiar, and we believe we already know, perhaps even *too well!* This is where observing facts and asking questions becomes critical. Being warm requires that we consciously *give* our time, energy, and whole-hearted attention to asking questions that reveal not just the *external* details of our mate's life, but also the *internal* thoughts and feelings that define desires, fears, needs, successes and failures that she *experiences* every day, and reveal her *unique* responses to the mystery of being alive.

In addition to internal *warmth*, we also need to define and provide *tenderness*. Warmth is an experience we all need every day, while tenderness is a more occasional experience that we need when experiencing emotional pain, self-doubt, frightening challenges, genuine loss, or maybe feeling sad or lonely with no identifiable reason or cause.

To offer the experience of tenderness, we must be willing to experience pain ourselves. Being vulnerable to pain, even someone else's pain, is something most of us are reluctant to experience. This natural reluctance to *willingly* make ourselves vulnerable to acknowledging, exploring, experiencing and learning from pain is the primary reason tenderness tends to be relatively rare.

When I was with Holly while she was going through her cancer treatments, I could see that her husband and friends were uncomfortable with the fact that she was ill. It is painful to experience someone so young being so sick, and possibly dying. So, rather than face our own pain and fear of death in order to share someone else's experience, we tend to ignore painful realities as much as possible. I could see that most people chose to stay away from Holly mentally and emotionally, and sometimes physically.

For Holly, the emotional isolation simply added to the

pain and terror of being ill. Seeing this process acted out was helpful for me in understanding how to give Holly the mental and emotional support, or *internal* tenderness she so clearly needed. I also had the opportunity to offer *external* tenderness by treating her radiated skin with the vitamin E and wheat germ oil.

Breaking open the vitamin E capsules one by one and applying the contents to her poor radiated skin required time and patience that she experienced as a prolonged act of tender concern. During this nightly ritual, we chattered about people, life, ourselves, the play she was in, and the entire experience was immensely comforting for us both.

To make this experience truly tender required that I be whole-heartedly present, fully relaxed, and happy with the moment. There could be no rush in my manner or thought to indicate I wanted to be somewhere else, or doing something different. Instead, to be genuine this experience had to be seen as the best and most satisfying moment possible, which required my mind to be whole-heartedly focused and innocently content.

The point here is that real tenderness must be offered in a mental and emotional context that is congruent with what is needed in the moment. We cannot be *going through the motions*, doing what we think we *should*, following a *form* of what we believe is right, or have an attitude of fulfilling our *obligations* and still offer true tenderness. In other words, tenderness requires consciousness and caring.

Part of the responsibility that goes with becoming a

satisfying mate, competent parent, or real friend is to pur-posefully master the skills required to offer emotional warmth and real tenderness to the people we love. Does it seem that skill and awareness is needed, or do you believe that good intentions and sentimental feelings are enough?

In normal life we rarely think about either warmth or tenderness precisely and in detail. Mostly, we assume that part of being a good person is that we are *naturally* warm and tender, and never give the issue a second thought; that is, until we have a close encounter with serious illness, emotional pain, or death. Then, we quickly learn how im-portant warmth and tenderness really are, and how rare.

The Power of Conversation

Sigmund Freud recognized the power of conversation and stunned the world with his *"talking cure* of hysterical paralysis." While no longer new, the power of *personal conversation* has not yet been understood or integrated into normal life. If the skill necessary to offer *satisfying personal conversations* were integrated into normal minds and lives, then we would all be more relaxed, internally satisfied, and competent than what is usually the case.

It is through conversation, first as children and then as adults, that our view of reality is confirmed or denied. It is also through conversation that our *self-image* is established, and we grow-up with a solid, or fragile *internal value*. In addition, through conversation our trust in people and life is either established and developed, or *squashed like a bug*.

In relationship with a mate, conversation is the key to whether we express and expand a passionate connection, or lapse into a mindless routine and passive lethargy. Of course, conversation is just the *medium*, the *message* has to come from an active and involved mind and emotions that consciously adopts a desire to express love, pursue truth, and experience beauty.

When it is our desire to express love and pursue truth, we put energy and attention into consciously choosing topics for conversation that are truly meaningful, and we work to make every conversation equal and reciprocal.

Consciously creating *personal conversations* is different from the reactive and *impersonal* conversations that typify the normal experience. For one, in *conscious conversations* we choose topics that address internal needs, hungers and potentials, as well as significant joys, sadness, losses and fulfillments. We also discuss nature, and the suffering and needs of other people.

Finally, we use conversation to learn about and explore the *traditional* worlds of beauty found in art, music and literature, in addition to *non-traditional* sources of beauty found in pursuing truth and expressing love.

Take a moment and think about your choice of topics in conversation. Do you purposefully ask your mate, children, or friends about their joys and sadness? For instance, are you willing to listen to a loved one's pains and share in them without offering solutions or advice? Do you have the skill and interest to ask intelligent questions that explore both the obvious and the mysterious? If not, what do you choose to talk about?

Answering these questions will provide insight into your mind and conversations. It is important to notice that your thoughts are revealed in your conversation. To anyone who knows how to listen, everyone is an open book that even strangers can glance into and read a page or two, and it can be very disconcerting to acknowledge that what we all like to imagine are private sanctuaries, our minds, are really open to public view!

<u>Sharing</u>

One essential purpose of adult relationships is to *share* the experience of being alive. As everyone knows, life is lonely and sharing conversations, tasks, recreational activities, books, movies, music, and nature to name a few is what we all want and need but rarely understand, or know in detail how to offer and receive.

Of course, the first step is to create a *conscious identity* where we become competent to feed and fulfill ourselves. This step is critical, and one we often skip as we hope that a relationship will fill-up our emptiness. As we have seen, failing to develop a conscious identity, and then wanting a relationship to not only relieve our *loneliness* but also cure our *internal emptiness* is one reason people often feel disappointed with each other, and is a common source of creating "irreconcilable differences."

Acknowledging this *first step* in building emotional

bonds, and that we must take it alone is critically important because it establishes a realistic expectation that we must learn how to *think, understand, and work* for our own internal development. With this awareness, it is not a leap to observe that we need to master the skills and awareness necessary to share internal and external dimensions of life with another person.

What I have seen in over thirty years of talking to people about relationships is that most people believe, some consciously, but most *unconsciously*, that if they are *in love* their relationship should be satisfying, *effortlessly*! This is a conspicuous example of an oft-repeated life lesson that says, "The *experience* of life often proves to be quite different from our *idea* of what we think it should be."

Two initial insights necessary to make relationships internally satisfying and emotionally bonded are one: the *purpose* of relationships is to *share, grow and give*; and two, our *responsibility* is to *think, understand, care and work*. With these insights firmly embedded, we will understand and be in harmony with what is needed, and we will be emotionally prepared to master our part. Once we have this internal foundation to build on, creating intimate emotional bonds is fairly easy.

The wonderful part of my relationship with Bev was the sheer quantity and quality of sharing we experienced. We shared conversation, diet, exercise, movies, music, books, nature, photography, and for a time it seemed we shared a purpose for living that made internal growth a top priority. It was the sharing that made our relationship possible, and it was the deterioration in our sharing that ended it.

Part of what went into building our bond is that each morning we shared a work-out followed by morning chores, breakfast drink, coffee, conversation and classical music. This daily ritual fed essential internal and external needs in a context of moving together in a delightfully satisfying and genuinely meaningful harmony.

The harmony we experienced in the morning ritual extended throughout the day in how we handled each chore, or discussed any issue; whether personal, world, or gossip. We also spent time in nature hiking, talking, and taking photographs and experiencing delight in being alive and together. The quality and extent of our sharing created a relaxed and satisfying experience. So, what happened?

In simple terms, our fundamental *life purposes* were not the same. My life purpose was clearly defined in that I was committed to constantly grow and change in the pursuit of answering my question, "What, if anything, will make human life internally satisfying and meaningful?"

At first, Bev tried to adopt this purpose, but eventually decided that it did not fit her and felt she needed to be alone to discover what did fit. Since Bev and I never discussed what happened in any detail, this is my reconstruction relying on the tidbits of information she has offered, as well as observing her actions.

Being with Bev and experiencing some real sharing,

and then abruptly separating with no discussion, created the greatest joy and most intense pain imaginable. Out of this searing crucible of joy and pain came many lessons that have been of immense value, and surprisingly, at least to me, have helped to answer my lifetime question.

Without the experience of being out of control in a dizzying height of joy and depressing depth of pain, I might not have acknowledged the simple self-evident fact that *expressing love, pursuing truth, and experiencing beauty* — when understood and integrated into everyday life — are indeed timeless steps to internal satisfaction and meaning.

It is my hypothesis that any couple who makes it their shared *primary life purpose* to master these three steps, and then follows through with committed actions will create a bonded relationship that is as satisfying and meaningful as any human relationship can be. Not only will their relationship be genuinely intimate and meaningful, their individual lives will also be as fulfilled as possible.

The job, if someone has the interest, is to test this hypothesis by studying my books until he understands them. This is the preparation necessary to observe everyday life, acquire the critical awareness and skills, and over time test whether or not my hypothesis fits with your experience.

Identity & Meaning

For most people, identity and meaning are invisible issues critical to their internal fulfillment, but beyond their training and awareness. As we have seen, *identity* is the *ultimate source* of our purposes and priorities, and if *normal*, creates a desire to control success, security, and approval. We have also seen that the issue of *meaning* determines whether our daily experience is filled with *enduring value*, or we allow life to slip away without purpose or point.

Together, our identities and the degree of meaning we create determine whether we become internally fulfilled, or experience life defined by everything from mild tension and discontent, to severe disappointment and depression. Given the consequences to daily life, it is amazing how little our species has learned about *identity* and *meaning*.

In this book, we have defined identity in enough detail to see the *universal* characteristics in *normal* vs. *conscious* identities, so we can see the *internal structure* that forms the core of everyone's character. In the process, we have learned that at the core, or base of a *normal* identity is fear, while the foundation of a *conscious* identity is desire, and each foundation provides strikingly different purposes, and different outcomes, or consequences.

It is important to see that I have presented *normal* and *conscious* as discrete and often contradictory perspectives. You may find that you are a complex mixture of normal and conscious characteristics, so for you the issue of identity may not be as simple as I make it appear.

As a result, your job is to thoroughly understand all the internal characteristics that define both *normal* and *conscious* identities, and then observe the details of your own mind, emotions, choices and behaviors to accurately see your *unique* combination of core characteristics. With this information, you are prepared to identify the precise skills and awareness you need to master, or can decide you are as conscious and internally complete as you want to be.

The critical issue is that to create internal meaning, we must first develop a *conscious identity,* and then master the ability to be authentic, original, and creative in our *unique* responses to being alive. It is also important to notice that everyone's core character and internal life is improved one *small piece at a time.* The same is true for external life.

Benjamin Franklin observed this fact over two hundred and fifty years ago when he acknowledged that daily life is improved by single increments. One example he used was noting that life in Philadelphia was significantly improved when raised wooden walkways were built on the sides of the main street where all the shops were. These *side*-walks meant that when it rained people did not have to slug their way through the mud to get from point A to B, which was a small but significant improvement.

I have seen many similar improvements in my lifetime. As a child, we literally had an *ice-box* for storing perishable food, and the *ice-man* came to our house two times a week to deliver a large block of ice. I remember he had a piece of leather thrown over his shoulder to protect him from the ice that he carried with a large set of tongs. For years into my adult life, and long after it disappeared into history, I would still call the refrigerator an *ice-box*. Very similar to what we do today when we call companies that produce CD's of modern music *Record* companies even though vinyl has not been mass produced for a long time.

Another example of an improvement to our external lives happened with cleaning clothes at home. When I was young, my mother had a wringer-washer. This machine was just an open tub with an agitator that moved the clothes around to wash them. The operator had to put each piece of clothing through the wringer to squeeze out the water and then hang the clothes on the line. When the automatic washer came out, and was soon followed by an electric or gas clothes-dryer, external life was immensely improved. I still greatly appreciate these improvements.

However, it must be noted that some people opposed even these improvements. For instance, some people felt that clothes dried in a machine did not smell as fresh as those dried outside on a clothesline. My thought is that the people who resisted the dryer probably never hung out clothes on a cold day in a Michigan winter, and then later had to take them down when each piece was frozen stiff!

My point here is that we frequently resist any and all change, so we can expect that we will be cautious or even suspicious of anything new, no matter how much it may improve our lives. Another point to observe is that improvements are *always incremental — never absolute or perfect*, in both internal and external experience.

Understanding Value

We have seen that part of a normal identity is a set of *universal purposes* that determine our priorities and values. This means that when it is our purpose to pursue approval, success, fitting-in so we can feel good about ourselves, security so we can feel safe, and entertainment so we can ensure pleasantness, then these *purposes* determine our everyday *priorities* and become what we *value*.

I observed a common example of normal purposes and priorities during a television tribute to John Denver shortly after he died in the crash of his light plane. The interviewer was asking Annie, his ex-wife, how she reacted to the news he had died. Her response was, "Well John had fun playing golf that morning, and was pleased with his score. He was generally feeling good about himself, and he was excited about his new plane." (The one that killed him!)

This response may have been one of the reasons they were divorced. However, assuming Annie was trying to be nice, she was revealing normal purposes and priorities and was showing that John's life was in order, he felt good about himself, he was having fun, and *that's what life's all about*. Bottom line she was sad he was gone, but happy he was having such a *good time*.

We are not here to evaluate John's life, but to understand Annie's description, and how she chose these things to say on national TV. At the least, she knows there is nothing bad in what she is saying, and she also knows she is saying things other people will probably agree define what in normal terms is seen as *a good life*.

In fact, what Annie was describing was a *pleasant* day, not a *meaningful* day. There is a difference. Pleasantness has value for a moment, but it does not last. This is an absolute statement but check it out against your own experience. Haven't you had many a day when you had fun, felt good about yourself, and were excited about something new — a boy/girlfriend, car, house, job, TV, etc.?

Have all your pleasant days added up to increasing your experience of internal meaning, or lasting value? Or, were they just pleasant days that slipped into history with no lingering significance or satisfaction? On the other hand, can you remember gaining a significant insight that changed how you see yourself, other people, or the facts of reality? What was the consequence — a flicker of pleasantness, or an experience of lasting satisfaction that brought with it a permanent increase of skill or awareness to your mind and emotions, and enduring value, or real meaning to your life and relationships?

This is a subjective choice, which means there is no way to *prove* one is the better than the other. We can observe, however, that with a *normal identity* it is neither our priority, nor is it in our awareness or skill set to express love, pursue truth, and experience beauty so every day we change in the depth and detail of what we understand, and as a consequence, constantly expand in the degree of our competence to nurture ourselves, other people, and nature.

If we choose to replace a *fear-based normal identity* with a *desire-based conscious identity,* then activities with built-in meaning become our primary purpose and daily priority. One consequence is that our lives inevitably grow in internal meaning as we age. It is my observation that with a normal identity we may be successful and have everyone's approval, and also fit-in at all the best places and with the best people, but this in no way means our lives will *expand* in value as we age, rather than *contract* and diminish.

It never helps to critically evaluate other people, but it does help to become more self-aware, so what do you see is true for you? Do your priorities lead to expanding your internal value, so your life increases in meaning with each day, or do you tend to protect, contract, and diminish?

The next important question, "Do you *care* if your life is meaningful?" Given the priorities of a normal identity, even thinking about meaning is rare, maybe when alone late at night and the distractions of the day have fled in the darkness and it becomes clear you are alive now, but not forever! Everyone suffers an occasional fleeting thought about meaning, but creating a *burning desire* to experience meaning is entirely different.

Ultimately, a *compelling desire* and *focused commitment* to master expressing love, pursuing truth, and experiencing beauty is necessary for all internal development.

Meaning Matters — For Young & Old

Two brutal facts are that life is a mystery and death is forever, and as a result, *meaning* matters more than anything else. People often choose to protect themselves with *fantasies,* rather than acknowledge the brutal facts, but they get old and die anyway. The most damaging consequence of living in a fantasy world is that we lose all opportunity to express love, pursue truth, and experience beauty.

In denying that life is a mystery and death is forever, we pretend that normal priorities and purposes are important, when in fact they only seduce us into spending our precious life's time on polishing images, protecting egos, pursuing security, and entertaining into oblivion.

A therapist, whom I have known for over 25 years and trained to do my work, decided to experiment with her daughter, son-in-law, and three grandsons by offering them classes in internal development. The family has gotten together on an irregular basis, usually on Sunday evenings, and she gives them lessons on *thinking for understanding, feeding internal needs, and building emotional bonds.*

During one session, Donna pointed out to her 11 year old grandson, Dallon, that in describing people, events, or experiences he focused on what was missing, or not there. She noted that when his attention was solely on the negative, or what was missing, his role was to always criticize. This role prevented him from seeing the positives, or even to allow the negatives to teach him what was needed.

She then observed that the ultimate consequence is he was *missing his life.* The next week, Dallon came back to the family meeting and announced that he did **not** want to miss his life, so he was going to *acknowledge and learn* from life's positives and negatives — and he proceeded to do just that! At school, his teacher observed that somehow Dallon had changed and now he is a "*...joy to be around.*"

In normal life, people rarely gain insight and change. Instead, it is far more common to gain insight and then procrastinate for months, years, or decades being insecure, afraid, anxious, or just waiting for more information so we can be absolutely certain that if we do change it won't hurt, and the benefits will be overwhelmingly advantageous.

When we acknowledge life's brutal facts, we no longer fear changing. Now, we are afraid of not changing, because we see life is short and experience an urgent desire to master love, truth, and beauty before we die. Take a moment, and observe your response to observations that reveal you need to change some part of yourself. Do you make the needed adjustments, or do you *meander* through time feeling no urgency, because there is *always tomorrow?*

Very recently at the family meeting, Donna first defined *meaning* as being created by experiences that have *lasting value,* and then went around asking each person what he/she felt was meaningful. Now 13, when it was Dallon's turn, he said the classes with Donna provided his *only* meaning. Then he began to cry, and continued to cry for about twenty minutes.

Dallon's mother also cried because she could see her son had internal needs she had not understood and could not feed. She also sees that her time with her son is really short, and is responding by using the time she still has to learn how to nurture both herself and her son, *internally*.

Everyone was taken aback by the strength of Dallon and his mother's response because the family is guided by normal purposes and priorities, so *meaning, love, truth and beauty* are not consciously engaged, clearly defined, or purposefully mastered. How about you and your family, do you consciously engage, define, and master love, truth, and beauty for the purpose of creating emotionally bonded relationships and internally meaningful lives?

Finally, in the most recent family session, Donna asked each person to define love, and Dallon said; **"Love is a connection that is deeper because of understanding."** What makes this definition significant is that at 13, Dallon took information that he got from his grandmother and put it together in a form that was not parroting what she had taught him, but was a new, original, and a creative expression that was authentically and uniquely his own.

The purpose of my work is to help people fulfill their potentials. This event with Dallon is a satisfying fulfillment of my life's purpose, in part, because at Dallon's age, I too was in need of someone to teach me about life's meaning. Another reason for my satisfaction was because Dallon did not *parrot my definition*, but created an authentic but still accurate *experiential definition* all his own.

<u>Fulfilling Our Unique Potentials</u>

Everything in Nature is happier when its potentials are fulfilled, and human beings are no exception. So if acorns can be happy, then every little acorn is happiest when it grows into an oak tree. By the same token, since human beings have the potential to become self-aware, life-aware, and other-aware, we will always be happiest when we integrate love, truth, and beauty into daily life.

It is important to take this statement as a hypothesis to test against your own experience. What you can see from Dallon's example is that at 13, he acknowledged that the only truly meaningful experiences in his life came from the classes his grandmother offered. This means he was aware enough to observe the need to fulfill his *internal* potentials, that his grandmother was his only source of information, and that he felt both sad and grateful.

In normal life, we are trained to care about things that do not exist, or do not matter. As a result, too often we spend our lifetimes pursuing security that does not exist; or approval, advantage, and entertainment that ultimately do not matter, and provide no lasting value or internal meaning. Without a doubt, we would all have significantly more satisfying and meaningful lives if we mastered both our *universal* and *unique* internal needs and potentials.

You may now want to ask, "Yes *but*, **how** do I master my internal needs and potentials." As usual, you ask truly important questions.

The absolute bedrock source for all internal growth is *observing* experience. One way to begin focusing our minds is to define significant life issues in *terms of experience* rather than as *concepts, beliefs, or feelings.* This is what my friend was doing with her family. For instance, Donna asked each person to define the words *love* and *meaning* in terms of their own experience. To help them in this task, Donna assisted in the process by offering an initial *working definition* of meaning as being any experience that results in providing *lasting value.*

In the **Foreword,** I provided *experiential definitions* for love, truth, and beauty. Later on, I added Anne Frank's definition for love, and then Dallon's. The point is that we need *working definitions* for love, truth, beauty, potentials, needs, purpose and meaning if we want to master the ability to integrate these experiences into everyday life.

Normally, we don't precisely define any critical topics, and even if we try, we do so in terms of beliefs or feelings, rather than *observable experiences.* One problem is this lack of connection makes it impossible to test for effectiveness, develop new awareness, or acquire new skills when our definitions are based on beliefs and feelings.

For instance, when we define love based on *sentimental intentions,* we can never identify in detail precisely what we must master to feed another person's internal needs so she will experience being loved. One consequence is that we forever fail to develop the awareness and skill necessary to become internally competent to offer real love.

On the other hand, using Dallon's definition, we can first define the word *understanding* in terms of experience, and then see whether or not we have the skill and awareness necessary to focus on another person, listen to his pains and joys (without offering advice or solutions), and then explore his experience with intelligent questions until we *understand* his perspective in detail.

If we can understand another person, not only to our satisfaction but also in the other person's mind as well, we can genuinely share life. We can also answer the question, "Does our connection seem deeper, warmer, and closer because of the shared understanding, or not?"

Answering this last question is how we test whether or not Dallon's definition of love holds true in the real world. Following the process of defining each issue in *terms of experience,* and then testing to see if what we expected actually happens is how we learn to define needs and potentials, and then master feeding and fulfilling them.

If we want to grow, this is the required process. Happily, this process is no *secret!* It is also not fast, easy, or effortless, but it is effective and will reward us with a lifetime of satisfaction and meaning. It is important to begin by taking each phrase—*expressing love, pursuing truth, and experiencing beauty*—and define each one in terms of real experience, or borrow my definitions while taking the time to understand each activity. Next, we test the working definitions against the facts and discover the consequences. Following this process, we eventually learn what is true.

Conscious Identity & Human Evolution

The normal adult response to being alive is to assume that we already know what the game of life is all about, and even if we don't know, we at least *pretend* to friends and family that we do. This attitude of feeling we already know, should know, or are entitled to pretend we know the answers to the mystery of life and death is supported by religious beliefs, new-age gurus, philosophers, experts, intellectuals, psychologists, and many people who have never observed a single reality, cracked a relevant book, or ever had a clear and conscious thought about anything.

One way to test this observation is to ask around and see how often people are quick to explain their opinions, and/or *answers* about life, versus how often people have *intelligent questions* they pursue over time patiently gathering insights they actually test against everyday experience.

What is your process? Do you have questions about needs, potentials, life, love, truth, beauty, and how to build emotional bonds, or do you rely on beliefs, feelings and answers? Or perhaps you ignore these issues hoping they will take care of themselves? In fact, throughout the whole of civilized history most people have lived and died blindly following cultural beliefs, while asking few questions.

As a result, people today do not understand any more about how to create internal fulfillment, raise a child with his self-worth intact, or how to build genuine emotional bonds than people at any other time in history.

Scientifically and technologically we have evolved, and it shows in the toys, tools, weapons, and conveniences we have today vs. three hundred years ago. However, look at the *core character* or *internal identity* of a normal person today vs. three hundred years ago and you will see remarkably little change. You will also see little change in the social, political, and economic problems of human beings today vs. human beings at any other time in history.

For example, throughout history the *many have always been exploited by the few*, and it is no different today. The methods change, but the process does not. Relying on military force to solve international conflict has not changed. Being externally motivated in our personal lives, while failing to define or understand our deepest internal hungers, needs, and potentials has also not changed, at least not in terms of what I have read in history and literature, or observed in my professional and personal experience.

Even scientific change has not happened easily. Instead, for thousands of years belief in religion, love of the status quo, fear, and short life spans restricted our ability to explore the natural world. Today, those same forces continue to restrict our exploration of our internal world.

It was the *scientific method* that eventually freed our minds to explore and discover nature. Now, we need to apply that same method to explore the internal world of our minds and emotions. If we do, there will be a similar observable result in that people will evolve in their ability to understand and nurture themselves, life, and each other.

Everything I offer is meant to open the door to observing the internal processes that define who we are now, and to offer options into seeing our ultimate potentials. The reason human beings are so primitive in overall internal development is the process we use. In exploring the natural world we learned to use the *scientific process*, but in learning about ourselves we still rely on superstitious beliefs and feelings, intellectual theories, and self-righteous judgments, just like we did throughout the dark ages.

If people would study the fears and purposes that define a normal identity, they would see their core characters are built on a primitive process that has proven over many millenniums to create prejudice, foolish judgments, ignorance, and an endless repetition of the same old mistakes.

On the other hand, if people would study the desires and purposes that define a *conscious identity*, and learn how to make even a few changes, they would discover the joy and pain of learning to see reality accurately, define all real needs, think for understanding, and become competent to nurture everything alive.

It is impossible to prove anything to a mind that is disconnected from reality and determined to follow its prejudice and ignorance to the grave. Recognizing the impossibility of proving anything to anyone, it has never been my purpose to proselytize. It is a waste of everyone's energy. So I offer my observation-based insights to see whether studying and learning this material can transform your understanding and develop your mind and emotions.

What I see for the future of human beings is that if we retain *normal identities,* then *fear and greed* will forever reign supreme, and the future will be a sad repetition of the past, only on a grander and more devastating scale. It has to be that way, a mathematical certainty if you will, simply because *purpose determines outcome*—and our *identities determine our purposes.*

If our identities do not change from normal to conscious, it is impossible for our purposes to change. The tragic reality is that we humans have proven beyond a doubt there is no political system, educational institution, or religious belief we cannot subvert and pervert with a normal identity. If we want the future to be an improvement over the past, then we must begin by creating new raw material—transforming our individual identities.

Changing our identities from normal to conscious is how to engage every human problem at its source, the core character of each person.

We cannot make changes by instituting another *system.* No religion, political structure or economic system will make any long-term life-affirming difference. Instead, we need to make the evolution of each individual our goal. Teaching the internal tools that free people from fear and greed and teach them to be competent to create satisfying and meaningful lives is the only option that will work long-term, because it is the only way people will be educated in how to fulfill their *universal* and *unique* potentials.

People who are trained to think clearly, care whole-heartedly, and master their internal needs and potentials will be authentic, original, creative, and fulfilled. Happy and fulfilled people will see reality accurately, clearly define the world's problems, and arrive at solutions they are internally prepared to implement cooperatively.

So if you are thinking, "This guy makes grandiose thinking look minor league!" you will get no argument from me. I am saying this is what is needed. I am not saying it is possible, frankly, I don't know. I rather doubt it, after all I may be grandiose, but I'm not crazy! Nonetheless, I can see what the future holds if we do **not** grow and change, not that many people I talk to seem to really care, but I do, and so I provide what is needed whether I have any real hope it will be acknowledged and applied, or not.

On the positive side, I have already seen that any individual who studies and learns even part of the information I offer will observably improve his or her life. I also know that anyone who masters this material will fulfill much if not all of his internal potential. Finally, I can predict with certainty that if most people on planet Earth developed *conscious identities* the world would be unimaginably different in a life-affirming, genuinely satisfying, and truly meaningful direction.

Of course, what I predict with certainty you are quite free to take with a *grain of salt and a barrel of humor*. On the other hand, you might test Hatherley's first principle of life that says *purpose determines outcome* and see whether or not this principle applies in your experience too.

When Beethoven's fifth symphony was first played the sound was unfamiliar to the music lover's ears of his time, and the story goes that one listener was exasperated by the length of Beethoven's coda, and is reported to have yelled, "Beethoven, for God's sake make it end!"

I guess Beethoven liked his great symphony and was in no hurry to end it. I think what this book offers is important, and I want other people to think so too, and taking my leave is suddenly, in this moment, more emotionally difficult and sad than I imagined it would be, or in the past it has been. I hope you learn something from reading this book that is useful to you, as well as your mate, family and friends.

Human beings may survive with normal identities, but they will **not** survive with meaning. Meaning requires a conscious identity, and integrating love, truth, and beauty. Here's wishing you a *meaningful* life. PH

Other Books by Dr. Hatherley

Developmental Tasks For Children, Adolescents & Adults: *A Full Picture of Internal Development from Self-Worth & Emotional Safety to Integrating Love, Truth, Beauty & Wisdom.* 147 pages.

The Internal Development Necessary to Become Loving & Wise: 141 Pages.

Choosing a Framework to Define Life: *Understanding Framework is the Magic Key to Understanding Individuals, Couples, Families, Cultures and the History of Human Civilization.* 141 pages

Timeless Lessons from a Well-lived & Loved Ordinary Life: *A Psychological Autobiography of an Ordinary Man with a Special Purpose.* (Estimated date of completion, January, 2015)

Master the Science of Living & Art of Being Happy, 184 pages.

Dr. Hatherley's books can be ordered online:

www.paulhatherley.com

Paul Hatherley

Part Three

Appendix—

Poems By Paul

Paul Hatherley

Introduction

In the movie, *My Fair Lady*, Rex Harrison played the role of Professor Higgins. Since it was a musical, Rex had to sing, the only problem being that he was not a singer. This fact created a potentially show-stopping problem, which a wise singing coach helped him resolve. She suggested that Rex not try to sing, but instead, just *talk in tune*. This is what he did, and the movie was a great success, even though the leading man, by his own admission could not sing!

A similar problem has happened to me. I do not know how to write poetry, but I can write in stanzas, eliminate punctuation, and as everyone knows, I have mastered incorrect grammar! The result is a small collection of what I am calling *poems*. You are quite free to call them whatever you want, but for the sake of identification if I say *poems*, you will know what I mean.

My original purpose for writing these poems was to illuminate life's basic facts, internal needs, primal experiences, and conscious responses that would be accurate and honest, personal, and might emotionally touch the reader. The job of each poem is to make the basic facts that define everyone's existence, as well as the internal needs and primal experiences necessary for satisfaction and meaning, become more intensely alive and viscerally real.

The first poem in this collection is, **Alive, Lost, and Alone — Somewhere in Eternity**. This poem sets the scene by describing the basic facts that define everyone's experience and predicament in being a live creature. First, read the poem, and then take a moment to think about what it says and means. Next, read the description that follows. Finally, *observe* your own experience so that you see the facts of life for yourself, note your *responses* to these facts, and then connect the *consequences*. What do you see?

Note To The Reader: I wrote the following poems and letter over a decade ago and first *Appended* them to one of my other books. As I continued to write new books, always experimenting, expanding, and making the information more detailed and experiential this Appendix eventually fell by the wayside and was no longer attached to a book.

Recently I reread the poems, decided they might have value, and chose to resurrect and attach them here. The poems and letter are very personal, and in some ways primal, so they actually fit with some of the stories and attitudes expressed in this book. I hope you find in their content useful insights and experiences. PH

Alive, Lost and Alone—
Somewhere in Eternity

I am an Ordinary Person
And Like every Ordinary Person
My Life has Two Critical Dates—
Birth Date & Death Date

Every Event, Small and Large
Before my Birth Date
Happened Without Me!

The Universe was Born
And Became Middle-Aged
Without My Guidance or Knowledge
Even Dinosaurs and a Whole Planet
Teeming with Animals, Birds, Fish
And Magnificent Trees
Was Born, Lived, Died
And Completely Passed Away
While I Knew Nothing of any Event
Large or Small

Then, My Parents, Speaking of Small Events
Met, Courted, Married & Copulated
And Still—I was Not There!
Finally, in Early February of 1945
I Appeared

Odd, Isn't it
That We Number the Years?
If We Didn't—We would see We are Lost!
By Assigning a Number to Every Year

Paul Hatherley

We Pretend to Know Where We Are
The Fact—However—Is We are All Lost
Somewhere in Eternity

As a Child, I Hoped I Was Not Alone
Sadly, I Slowly Learned that My Parents
Neither Saw nor Cared About
My Thoughts or Feelings
And Did Not Understand Internal Needs

Now, I See I am Lost in an Ocean of Time
And I am Utterly Alone!
The Reality is Terrifying—
But There is No Escape
These Facts Are the Mystery of Being Alive
And Require My Acknowledgment & Response

Reluctantly, I look thru a Veil of Fear
And See That for the Universe
Time is Measured in Infinite Quantities
Totally Beyond My Experience
But In My Little Life
Time is Measure in Small Quantities
All Too Easy to Measure

This Only Means that the Universe
Can Afford to Meander through Time
Without a Single Priority or Purpose
Where My Moments are Numbered
And Constantly Diminishing

Which Means I Need to Clearly Define
Every Priority and Purpose

If I want to Experience
Lasting Satisfaction & Permanent Meaning

Responding to the Need to Earn My Keep—
And Pay for The Privilege of Being Alive
I Have Learned to Give Undivided Attention
To Every Fragile & Fleeting Moment
Whether Painful—Pleasurable—Or Neutral

By Paying Constant Attention
And Never Protecting the Status Quo
With My Ideas, Feelings, Judgments or Beliefs
I Have Innocently Received & Responded
To All of Life's Beauty & Ugliness

My Only Purpose is to Fully Experience
Learn From, Be Changed By, And Over Time,
Actually Understand & Nurture
Myself, Other People, & Nature

PH—2000

The normal response to being alive, lost, and alone is to deny all three, and then we hasten to explain away these scary and emotionally painful facts. As a result, rather than acknowledge that life is a mystery and fails to come with a map or owner's manual, we normally respond by denying these inconvenient facts. Instead, we acquire a philosophy, religion, belief system, or enough distractions that we avoid being aware of any painful or frightening fact that might confront us with the mystery of being alive.

Of course, nothing scares us more than *feeling alone*. All we need is to look at the *fact* that each person is born alone and dies alone to see that in spite of how we *feel*, the *fact* is each one of us must swim across the river of life all by ourselves. Being responsible to swim the river of life alone is not optional, even though we often like to pretend that we are *one with the universe*, that God will protect us, or that a sentimental belief will somehow make this observable fact disappear.

Mental and emotional development begins with acquiring an innocent curiosity and burning desire to see reality accurately, no matter where the facts lead. One place to start is by acknowledging the obvious fact that we are each **Alive, Lost, and Alone—*Somewhere in Eternity***. Then, we see that human beings are not *one with the universe* in at least one self-evident and very significant way. That is, the universe has an infinite quantity of time to meander through its development, but each person has a finite life span, so no human being has the luxury of being able to meander aimlessly through his/her days.

A *conscious* response to life span is to acknowledge that we care about satisfaction and meaning, and we want to fulfill our potential to be a consciously content person who is also a satisfying mate, competent parent, and real friend. Contrast this *conscious* purpose with the *normal* purpose to pursue success, security, approval, and pleasant feelings until death unexpectedly rings the bell, and we are gone.

The Experience of Being
Touched, Taught & Changed
By Every Breath

Being Aware of One Breath
Constantly Following Another
Makes Being Alive Stunningly Real—
Until, Over Time, It Becomes Evident
That the Whole Complex Weight
Of Our Own Unique Existence
Hangs Precariously
On the Slender Thread of One Breath
Relentlessly Following Another

Finally, When Our Breathing Fails
And The Fragile Thread Breaks
Shockingly, Our Lives Instantly Contract
And Disappear Down One Final Sigh

If While Our Breath is Strong
Our Minds are Content to be Absorbed in Trivia
We May Survive for a Normal Life-span
But We Never Experience Being Alive

There is a Whole World
Of Needs, Truth, Lies, Beauty, Ugliness
And Other Breathing Creatures
That We Must See, Understand & Nurture

Paul Hatherley

Before We Can Say with Confidence
"Yes, I Know Life!"

Consciousness is Born
And Real Living Begins
With Being Aware that One Breath
Constantly Follows Another
Until We Feel a Cold Chill
At the Base of Our Spines that Says
"I Really Am Alive!"

Upon This Innocent but Chilling Awareness
An Authentic & Original Human Life
Can Finally be Built
Breath by Breath
And Observation by Observation
With One Insight Following Another
Until the Whole World is Seen & Understood
And Added to Our First Startling Realization
"I am Alive!"

Finally, With a Conscious Mind & Emotions
Each Breath Teaches Us Something New
About the Experience of Being Alive
And Each Insight into Being Alive
Changes One Thread Of
Our Consciousness
Forever!

PH—2000

In normal life, we like to believe security is possible, and that being alive is not dangerous, risky, and uncertain. In the process of trying to feel safe, we lose the intensity and passion created by innocently acknowledging the risk and adventure that always accompanies just being alive.

If we see that every second our lives hang precariously by the thread of one breath following another, we create a constant reminder that being alive is risky and terrifyingly impermanent. Acknowledging that life is fragile can prevent us from lapsing into the normal state of complacency, entitlement, or oblivion that often defines our daily lives.

Once we accept that life is precarious and fragile, it is time to observe our surroundings. To see life accurately, however, we have to admit that we are separate from everything else in the universe. In normal life, we usually won't tolerate acknowledging our total separateness. As a result, people often *distort reality* by relying on a belief or feeling they are *one with the universe* rather than *acknowledge* the *facts* by making accurate observations and asking honest questions. After distorting reality, we can never understand ourselves — or our children, mate, and friends.

By contrast, in becoming conscious we want to develop our minds and emotions until we genuinely understand and are competent to nurture ourselves and other people. In the process, we see that we are only an insignificant dot in a vast and complex mystery. Since the world is vast, fulfilling our potential to understand requires we learn how to be *touched, taught, and changed* by every breath.

Ordinary Sex
For a Conscious Couple

We Begin Innocently
Our Only Intention
Is to Talk About Ordinary Life
Our Honest Responses and Real Needs

Our Purpose is a Mutual Desire
To Understand the Unique Mysteries
Of Each Other's Experience

So with Focused Attention
And Whole-hearted Caring
I Look into Your Eyes
And Listen to Your Words
While You Paint Pictures
Of Your Unique World
In My Mind & Memory

I See You as You are Now
And as You Have Been
I See Your Mind and Emotions
As They Have Grown and Changed
I See Your Longing, Hunger and Pain
And Every Innocent Delight & Joy

Our Conversation Flows as Effortlessly
And Innocently as Fresh Water
Flowing with Clear Purpose
Down a Sunny Mountain Slope

There is Nothing Missing or Incomplete
Our Satisfaction Fills all Emptiness
My Eyes Lightly Hold Yours
And You Softly Return My Gaze

Now, Responding to the Warmth
And Affection We Have Created
Our Lips Meet—and Melt
Into a Deep Celebration
Of the Mystery of Life in You
Touching the Mystery of Life in Me

Again and Again
My Kisses Play Across Your Lips
Your Breath Sweetens
And I Know There is No Experience
More Satisfying than one Simple Kiss

In the Fullness of the Moment
Surprisingly, And Without Calculation
We Begin Touching
Simply and Innocently
Our Only Purpose is to Extend
The Experience of Each Other
Thru a Conscious and Sensual Touch

Paul Hatherley

Our Clothes Provide an Easy Obstacle
Quickly Overcome—Until Finally
With Every Cell Tingling
Skin Meets Skin

The Moment Arrives when Our Desire
Demands That My Body Enter Yours
And in That Fragile Fleeting Moment
We are Aware of Our Separateness &
Our Intimately Personal Connection

We Feel Both Joy and Sadness
In Being Alive and Alone
And so Briefly Together
In Just Moments We Can No longer
Discern Who is Inside Whom
We Know Only That We are Together

Somehow Orgasms Happen—or Not
We Do Not Care
Our Fulfillment was Complete
With Conversation & Expanded by Our Kisses
And We Were Changed by Touching
That Melted Two Unique Lives
Into One Egoless Experience
Where For One Moment
We Shared the Mystery
Of Being Alive

PH—1999

In this poem, we see the direct consequences of internal development as it affects the attitudes and actions of an ordinary couple. We see, for instance, that each person's *purpose* is to *give* energy and attention, while *sharing* experience. Following this purpose, the couple builds a bridge of intimacy across the canyon of separateness.

They do not wallow in silly sentiment, or try to build a superficial ecstasy based on a pretend world where they deny reality. Instead, each person is vulnerable to their own and the other person's internal hunger to experience a satisfying and meaningful conversation about real facts, personal responses, consequences, and internal needs.

Their conversation builds an intimate mental and emotional bridge to one another that opens the door to a reciprocal desire to experience conscious and personal touching and kissing. By feeding *old hungers,* our couple creates *new longings*, and they build an innocent intimacy that expands from one moment to another, always full of caring. They focus full attention on one moment at a time, and their responses are always open and honest, never controlled.

As the intensity of our couple's experience builds, it becomes natural, and even necessary to become sexual. Still, sex is not the central issue, or our couple's primary purpose. Instead, the desire to give and share personal conversation and conscious touch, while being grateful for the time together is all that really concerns either person. Sex is just one small part of the larger and more satisfying experience of giving and sharing conversation and touch.

One consequence of relying on the structure provided by a conscious purpose is that our couple experiences an indelibly satisfying moment, which they burn into their minds and memory because it feeds old hungers and new longings alike. This is a quintessential moment, and there is nothing better. We can never control the moment to *get* this experience; it can be ours only after acquiring internal development and becoming innocent and authentic.

Great Sex
For A Normal Couple

We Begin Manipulatively
And Our Primary Intention
Is to Get Approval & Pleasure
In Other Words
Feed Our Egos & Gain Advantage!

Our Unconscious Purpose is a Mutual Desire
To "Get" As Much as Possible
While "Giving" As Little as We Can
Which Means Our Attention is Divided
And Our Feelings are Empty Sentiment

We Chatter about Trivial Events
And Gossip Smugly About Other People's
Inadequacies and Misfortunes
Until Finally, Bored and Desperate
We Kiss

Your Breath Reflects the Anxious Tension
Boiling in Your Stomach
Mine, The Internal Battle Between
Two Hot Dogs & Three Brewskis

In Spite of the Odor
We Power Through Three Kisses

Paul Hatherley

And Move On
The Passion is Now Building
We Know because You are Breathing Hard
And There is a Heavy Sweat on My Brow
And Under My Arm Pits

Now—Sweating and Panting
The Orgasm Already in Sight
We Move into Position

You Direct My Every Move
In Time, My Index Finger is Numb
And My Mouth is Permanently Puckered
I Fear That I May Need Plastic Surgery
But Take No Heed Because My Turn is Coming

With all My Efforts You are Still Frustrated
Every Time You Almost Succeed
I Stop To Regain Feeling
Finally, With Your Scream of Relief
I Know It's Over and Now It's My Turn

You're Thinking How Glad You Are
That My Part is Quickly Accomplished
So You Only Have to Pretend
Interest For a Short Time
Now, Relieved and Drained it is Over
And We Both Protest How Great

Our Sex Really Is
And as We Say Goodnight
We Both Hasten to Say
"I Really Enjoyed Myself"
"We Must do This Again Sometime!"

PH—1999

It was far more fun to write the poem about ordinary sex, but we need the poem on great sex to provide contrast. While some parts of the story about great sex may be exaggerated, they are not nearly as extreme, or far from the mark of normal experience as people might like to believe. Both poems are not just about sex. Rather, they reveal our purpose for living, and our attitudes toward life, needs, and responsibility. If you observe life in the United States, or anywhere else on the globe, you will see that the normal purpose of human beings is to get through their life spans as comfortably and pleasantly as possible.

Rarely do people have enough internal development to adopt conscious purposes to give energy and attention, fulfill their internal potentials, and become competent to feed internal needs. One consequence of not having *conscious purposes* is that our individual lives are often as self-absorbed, superficial, pretentious, and as empty of satisfaction and meaning as the experience of our poor deprived and manipulative couple trying to **get** Great Sex.

The Experience
of Longing

All My Life I Have Longed For
One Opposite Sex Mate
And One Same-sex Friend

At First, My Desire Seemed
So Simple & Innocent
That with Conscious Effort
And Whole-hearted Caring
It Should be Easy to Satisfy

Over Time, However, I Learned
Precisely What was Needed to Be
A Satisfying Mate and Real Friend
And Suddenly, What Seemed Simple
Mushroomed into Something That Now
Seems Like it May Be Impossible

The Problem is That Being
A Satisfying Mate—or Real Friend
Requires Internal Development
This Means That One Pre-requisite
For Bonded Love and True Friendship
Is That Both People Must be Conscious
Enough to See Reality Accurately

Which in Part, Requires Acknowledging
That Every Person is Utterly Alone
And Absolutely Responsible
In a World Where if Love is To Exist
Each Person Must Contribute
Whole-hearted Caring

What I Have Found is That Everyone
Is So Terrified of Just Being Alive
And So Desperately Wants Someone Else
To Contribute the Energy & Attention
That Few Minds and Emotions
Are Developed Enough to Be
A Satisfying Mate or Real Friend

Instead, Everyone Wants to Find
The Right Mate—Or Friend
While Assuming He Can do His Part
The Only Question Anyone Asks
"Can My Mate or Friend Satisfy Me?"

Surprisingly—Being A Competent Mate
Begins with Seeing Life's Basic Facts
Like the Fact We are All Born
With A Mind, Body and Emotions
And That Lifespan Limits our Time
To Be Alive

Consciously Acknowledging Facts
And Seeing Reality Accurately
Provides an Honest Foundation
To Build Our Lives & Relationships

Without This Foundation All We Have
Are Sentimental Feelings And
A Desire for Advantages

If we Build Our Lives & Relationships
On Observing Facts & Feeding Needs
We Can Be a Satisfying Mate
And Real Friend

PH—2000

In this poem, a universal longing is defined, which we all share to one degree or another. We see this longing in children who jealously guard their *playtime* with friends. Teen-agers too, are often addicted to *hanging-out* with their friends, and are desperate to possess the *right* romantic partner. Finally, adults spend time and effort searching for a mate, and try to create intimacy and meaning that will endure over time, which given the divorce statistics now appears to be a nearly impossible task.

The problem is that in normal life we never learn how to build bonded relationships. As a result, we need training before we can become competent to do our part to give the conscious caring and focused attention that building an emotional bond requires. With conscious training, every-one can become a satisfying mate and real friend.

A significant part of becoming a competent adult is to be vulnerable to the pain of internal hungers, master feeding all our own needs, and then offer what we want to receive with no *expectation* that anyone reciprocate, ever!

It takes courage to acknowledge that we long for experiences we may never receive, and then, consciously offer what another person needs realizing in advance that our gifts may never be reciprocated. Being vulnerable to pain, responsible to offer what we want to receive, and aware that we may never have a mate or friend is all part of the process of becoming a competent adult.

In the normal world, we try to get other people to feed our hungers. This is one reason we spend so much energy on trying to acquire the *right* mate, and so little on being a satisfying mate or real friend. The only effective prescription for building an emotional bond in any relationship is internal development, and the description of longing in this poem offers genuine insight into what is painfully true and desperately needed.

Letter to Dad

Father's day is sometime soon, I'm not sure just when, and it gives me an opportunity to put into words my feelings about what it has been like for me to be your son.

In all our lives, we never had a conversation about us. In fact, we never acknowledged in any direct way that you are my father, and I am your son. Now, I am solidly into middle age (that is if I live to be 90), and you are inexorably into old age, so it is time for me to say directly to you what our relationship has meant to me. It seems appropriate that in 45 years, we should have one experience, even though one-sided and through a letter, that has some small degree of life-affirming meaning.

When I was a child, you seemed all-powerful, unapproachable, and perfectly competent. I wanted to be like you, but never felt I could be as competent as you. Every moment I could get positive attention from you was precious, and your criticism and disdain were devastating. I remember vividly every second we spent together. It isn't hard because they were few and far between. Nonetheless, I valued and felt grateful for each moment.

It was also true that I never felt good-enough to be your son. It just seemed to me that I was born with some fatal flaw in my character that I was powerless to change, which made me unworthy of you. You helped me understand this feeling the day I asked you how you saw me as a child, and you said, "You could never do anything right!" That one sentence summarizes how I have 'felt' about myself for much of my life. I have had a deep conviction that who I am, could never be *right*.

As an adolescent, I still saw you as being competent, and a 'good' man. Always better than me. At the same time, I still wanted you to be interested in me, to care about what I did, to be pleased or supportive. Again, I wanted to spend time together, to learn from you. What I experienced was that you would use me to accomplish tedious tasks, but would never bother to teach me anything.

For instance, when you rebuilt car engines, you had me hand grind the valves. One time I was grinding away while you talked to Paul C. teaching him how the engine worked. You never once attempted to say anything to me about the workings of internal combustion engines.

Of course, why should you talk to a son who could never do anything right? In terms of spending time together, we have gone on one hike and to one football game, and that is all the time we spent together for my entire adolescence. In fact, in terms of doing anything just you and me, that is it for my lifetime.

The message you have given me is clear. You simply are not, were not, and never will be interested in knowing me, spending time with me, or even acknowledging that I am your son. I doubt you realize this, but in 45 years you have never once asked me how I am doing, praised an accomplishment, offered a single word of encouragement.

Your function has been to provide criticism or disdain. To quote Mom from one discussion about my adolescence, which I am quite certain that you heartily agree with, "We wanted to approve of you — you just never did anything we could approve of!" In the past, when I stated these *facts*, your reaction would be to either criticize me further, or just complain that I never approved of you and never showed an appreciation for what you provided. I often wonder who was the parent, and who was the child?

So what was it like for me to want a relationship with you, to want your acknowledgment, to spend time with you, to be of value to you? It was relentlessly painful for me. I hated myself for not being worthy of your liking and respect. When my self-hatred became too much to bear, I was angry and defensive. I did what I could to get the material things that I hoped would provide some warmth and comfort. The surfboard, contact lenses, a car. Whatever I bought was an attempt to feed my needs and enhance life.

Certainly, you made it clear that whatever you gave me was out of fulfilling an obligation, and you never expressed anything but reluctance in anything you gave or permitted. Asking for anything from you was humiliating, because I had to endure your hesitant reluctance to give. In a lifetime, I cannot remember you giving a single thing with pleasure in your tone, face, or words. It was a painfully clear, consistent message about how little I meant to you, and how unworthy a son and human being I must be.

Throughout this time, I wanted to find some way to

have a relationship with you. To find a way to share experience, time, and maybe even real warmth or affection. In a lifetime, you never directly expressed the slightest degree of warmth or affection. For me, I simply could not face your disdain, criticism, or rejection to show you how much I admired you, loved you, and wanted to be like you.

Now, at 45, most of what I wanted from you, as well as the pain I received from you has faded. I no longer take your criticism and rejection seriously or personally. I see that you are fatally disconnected from your own life and feelings, and are isolated from everyone you have been linked to through blood or marriage. I wonder; do you have any awareness of what you have lost? You have lived a whole lifetime with much you might have given: warmth and affection you could have both offered and received, and you have experienced none of it.

God knows you have done your duty, fulfilled your obligations, followed the rules, and done the 'right' thing. He also knows there was little love in anything that you did, no joy or understanding, but much fear! While each person lives alone and dies alone, it is also true that you have taken the experience of isolation, separateness, and a gross uncaring and lack of consciousness to its outer limit. I wonder if you have any 'feeling' for at least a grain of truth in anything I am saying? I'm sure I'll never know.

On the positive side, (bet you thought we would never get here!) I learned from my image of you to respect competence. As a result, I am a competent man. In response to your being cold and unresponsive and the pain it caused me, I have learned how to be warmly responsive to others.

Learning from you how awful it is to be invisible and unimportant, I have learned how to give other people undivided attention and genuine understanding. Having suffered simplistic judgments and contradictory rules applied without thought or caring, I have learned to help other people understand themselves and life, including their inadequacies, with the purpose of feeding their needs.

I have also learned to accept you and feel compassion for your pain. I see that your drinking, for instance, is an escape from hungers that you deny or avoid, but now and then break through your defensive walls and become unbearable. I know you did your best, and in some ways just did to me what was done to you. There was nothing personal in it. You could not connect with me because you cannot connect with reality or yourself. You haven't a clue as to what your own needs are, and cannot imagine the hungers or needs of another person. All that you have ever valued is to survive and *be right*. In both pursuits, fear has been your primary motivator, and you have lived a life of silent emptiness and fearful desperation.

It is simply one of those normal tragedies that we are bound by blood, but nothing else. I'm sad for both of us.

PH-1990

Discussion of Dad's Letter

As the title stated, this is a letter not a poem. I am including this personal communication because it clearly identifies universal hungers, offers an example of how to illuminate painful experiences, and shows how to respond to disappointment and rejection with an attitude of wanting to understand and be responsible.

In acknowledging some universal pains and needs in a parent/child relationship, each reader has an opportunity to compare his/her response to similar experiences. For instance, if you observe the picture of this father-son relationship, then you can define more clearly what you experienced with your parents, what you would like to offer your children, and perhaps, what you would like to avoid.

One of the consequences of writing this letter was that my father never did acknowledge receiving it. My mother reluctantly acknowledged receiving the letter, and had one comment, which she delivered in a tone of condescending complaint. "You never did think we did anything *right*." In addition to the humorous irony of her comment, I could see that from her perspective the letter was about her, which was congruent with her perspective about life. That is, every event was always about her and her feelings. There was no other possibility.

This is a normal attitude, and is an inevitable consequence of never acquiring enough internal development to acknowledge that we are mentally, emotionally, and physically separate from other people, and responsible to feed and fulfill all our own needs and potentials. Nor, do we normally take responsibility to understand another person.

The only antidote to the terminal limitations imposed by the child-like self-absorption that dominates almost every normal mind is to first define mental and emotional development, and then commit the time and effort necessary to understand and master this conscious alternative.

Of course, whether to pursue internal development is a decision each person must make alone, even though the consequences of our decision will apply to ourselves, as well as anyone we want to love, or who wants to love us. The benefit of being alive right now is we have a choice to grow, or not. In our human past, there was no clearly defined conscious option, and as a result, no choice.